T0329302

MARKETS AND MEN

MARKETS AND MEN

A Study of
Artificial Control Schemes in some
Primary Industries

BY

J. W. F. ROWE, M.A.

Fellow of Pembroke College and
Lecturer in Economics in the
University of Cambridge

CAMBRIDGE
AT THE UNIVERSITY PRESS
1936

CAMBRIDGE
UNIVERSITY PRESS

University Printing House, Cambridge CB2 8BS, United Kingdom

Published in the United States of America by Cambridge University Press, New York

Cambridge University Press is part of the University of Cambridge.

It furthers the University's mission by disseminating knowledge in the pursuit of education, learning and research at the highest international levels of excellence.

www.cambridge.org
Information on this title: www.cambridge.org/9781107675001

First published 1936
First paperback edition 2014

A catalogue record for this publication is available from the British Library

ISBN 978-1-107-67500-1 Paperback

CONTENTS

MAPS

ILLUSTRATIONS

PREFACE

In the spring of 1935, Mr J. Jewkes of the University of Manchester and myself gave a series of wireless talks for the British Broadcasting Corporation under the title of "Markets and Men". These talks dealt very generally and summarily with the existing position and problems of a number of the world's primary industries. Neither Mr Jewkes nor myself felt desirous of publishing these talks as a series in book form, while any idea of writing jointly a more full and thorough survey of the world's primary industries was for various reasons impracticable. Ultimately, however, it was agreed that I should utilise the material embodied in the talks which I myself had given, in writing a study of the development of artificial control in the primary industries during recent years, both from realistic and also theoretical points of view. Chapters II, VI and VII, and parts of chapters IV and VIII are substantially a reproduction of my wireless talks, though of course brought up to date and modified accordingly: the remainder of the book is new, though I have, with Mr Jewkes' kind consent, made extensive use in chapter V of the two talks which he gave on cotton, and some use of the talk on wheat in which I was assisted by Mr R. B. Bryce. The writing of the book was finished during September 1935, and I must ask the reader to remember that the text bears that date, though short postscripts have been added to certain chapters in the revision of the final proofs during December 1935.

My interest in the problems of artificial control in the primary industries dates back, however, beyond the last twelve months. I first began to pay special attention to this subject in 1927, and during the years 1929–31 I was able, as a Fellow of the Rockefeller Foundation, to visit the United States, Cuba, Hawaii, British Malaya, Java and Brazil. This not only enabled me to learn something about the technique of a number of primary industries, but also to obtain first-hand information as to the points of view of the actual producers and their governments, thus supplementing the information obtainable in London which necessarily tends to be coloured by the financial and merchanting points of view. On returning from these travels, I wrote three detailed reports on sugar, rubber and coffee, which were published by the London and Cambridge Economic Service and circulated by the Royal Economic Society to its members, and also some articles dealing with the general economic principles of artificial control. For the comprehensive study of the whole subject which I still contemplate, I am clear that the time is not yet ripe, and that it is most unlikely to become so in the near future. On the other hand, I am equally clear that everyone, whether politician, business man, economist, or mere consumer, ought to pay more heed to this new development in industrial organisation, and also that a useful interim report on the subject can now be written. In this small book I have attempted such an interim report, and nothing more. I have intentionally retained the conversational style of my wireless talks, and have attempted to continue the same style throughout the book, because I am not writing primarily for my fellow-economists but for my fellow-citizens: at the same time I trust that the former will find matter which is not without some interest to them, especially in the later chapters.

If I were to acknowledge my obligations to all those persons at home and abroad—politicians, civil servants, economists, producers, merchants and manufacturers—who during the last eight years have given me substantial assistance in my studies of primary industries and of the whole problem of artificial control, this book would be several pages longer. I feel sure, however, that they all know how much I appreciate the generous help which they so freely gave me. Any selection from their ranks is as difficult as it is invidious, but I feel I must acknowledge my very special indebtedness to Mr Wykeham Price, Mr George Rae and Mr Charles Schulman.

J. W. F. ROWE

PEMBROKE COLLEGE
CAMBRIDGE

December 1935

Chapter I

THE ORIGIN AND GROWTH OF
CONTROL SCHEMES

THIS Jubilee Year has naturally given rise to re-
trospective stocktaking of the changes during the
last quarter of a century in every aspect of the national
life of Great Britain. Any comparison of the past and
present conditions under which we produce or purchase
our supplies of foodstuffs and raw materials, must however extend the process of reflection to international or
world developments, and all nations will indeed profit
if they use the occasion of the British Jubilee to reflect
upon the many great and significant changes which
have overtaken the world's primary industries during
the last twenty-five years. These include radical changes
in the main sources of supply, the mechanisation of
production in innumerable forms and the application
of science in innumerable ways, and the effects on
demand of rising and falling standards of living and
altered social habits and customs. But there has been
one truly revolutionary change, namely the evolution
of collective conscious control of supplies by the producers in a very large number of these industries; or
to put it in more everyday language, the appearance
of restriction and valorisation schemes, not only of
national, but also of international or even world-wide
extent. Here is no mere extension, or quickening of

previous development such as are the other changes: here is something which is so fundamental and so novel as genuinely to merit the adjective revolutionary, and so vigorous in its growth as to command our utmost attention.

Twenty-five years ago anyone who prophesied that the world supply of most of the important primary products would be subject to artificial control as the result of agreements between the producers or their governments, would not have commanded one minute's attention from economists or business men, politicians or statesmen. It is true that there had been a few such attempts with aluminium and zinc, and with agricultural commodities of relatively minor importance such as Greek currants; and though the great Brazilian coffee valorisation scheme of 1907 was still in operation, most observers considered it a final object lesson in the economic absurdity of all attempts to "interfere with the laws of supply and demand". It is true, also, that international agreements to control the supply of manufactured goods were by no means unknown, e.g. the International Steel Rails Agreement, and that monopolistic combinations of national extent in manufacturing industries were common, and increasing in number and efficiency every day. But to argue from this that similar attempts at collective control would shortly appear in the primary industries, would have been met with the scornful rejoinder that industrial organisation and the general conditions of production in the primary industries were entirely different, at any rate in agricultural industries. How could the million or so growers of American cotton, or the innumerable growers of wheat or sugar all over the world be organised to operate any common policy? And even if collective organisation were possible, and the attempt were made to dispense with the services of the middleman as the Brazilians had done, how could the producer gain? The middlemen knew their part of the business far better than any producers' organisation could, and competition ensured that producers got the highest possible price and consumers the lowest possible. Producers who tampered with the laws of supply and demand would get exactly what their stupidity and pig-headedness deserved, while if governments stepped in, the penalty would be doubled.

There are to-day certain economists, some business men and a few politicians who still hold essentially these views. Secondly there are a few economists, a great many business men, and probably a majority of politicians who are unreservedly in favour of artificial control, as compared with a purely individualist system of production and distribution, and in whose eyes "restriction for all and everything" is a panacea for the world's present troubles. But there is also a third party, larger than either of these, consisting of those who recognise the short-comings of individualist *laissez-faire* under present economic conditions, but cannot persuade themselves that schemes for the artificial control of the production or accumulated stocks of primary products are always economically sound and desirable, or always practicable, especially if the long-run as well as the short-run results are taken into account. And finally all these three parties are heavily outnumbered by those who do not feel that they can be bothered to take an intelligent and independent interest in these problems, either because they think that whatever happens can make little or no difference to themselves, or because they think that these problems are too complicated for the mere "man in the street". But the attitude of this great majority in so far as it is based on the former ground—that they themselves are little affected by the revolutionary change in the organisation of the supplies of primary products—is based on a delusion. Every one of us is interested as a consumer. The price of wheat, sugar, coffee or tea is what it is to-day, largely because of the measures of artificial control over supplies which have been taken in the recent past or are still in operation. These foodstuffs are consumed more or less in the state in which they are produced, but the price of raw materials like cotton, rubber, copper and tin are equally reflected, though perhaps less directly, in the price of clothes and cotton goods of all kinds, in the price of motor cars and motor transportation, in the price of supplies of electricity, in the price of tinned foods, and in the prices of the innumerable other things which require these raw materials for their manufacture. Of course, if the cost of one of these raw materials forms only a very small part of the final price of a commodity or service to the consumer, the effect on that final price may be small or for a time even indistinguishable, but that does not alter the fact that many little changes may make a very appreciable total difference to our standard of life and general well-being. Moreover, our interest as consumers is only one side of our interest. We may be also considerably interested as distributors of these foodstuffs, or as manufacturers of these raw materials, or we may be interested as investors in the business of producing them here in England or in other countries. Again, our individual fortunes may be vitally affected by the results of artificial control schemes on the incomes of the producers here or abroad, who buy goods by the making and selling of which we in turn obtain our incomes. I need not dilate further on the fallacy that we as individuals are not affected by the organised policies and operations of the producers of foodstuffs and raw materials, and that it is no concern of ours whether Brazil destroys its coffee crops, or whether the price of tin or rubber is doubled, or whether Great Britain and the United States grow their own sugar and thereby bring ruin on countries, like Cuba, which previously supplied them. And it is precisely because we are all so much affected in one way or another by the conditions which are governing the supply of foodstuffs and raw materials, that the excuse of the "man in the street" is not sufficient. These problems are complicated—there is no denying that—but so are many other of the problems of our daily lives on which we all have to make decisions, however incapable or unworthy we may feel ourselves to be. And we all have to make decisions concerning the organisation of the world's supplies of primary products—it is not merely the business men directly concerned who must do so—for since governments now play so large a part in these matters, all of us must decide as voters and tax-payers.

The following chapters attempt to give a general account of the recent history of six of the more important primary industries which have adopted artificial control schemes, special attention being paid to the causes which led to the establishment of these schemes, their general character, the changing policies adopted, the nature of the results achieved, and the reasons for their success or failure. But before we embark on these studies of individual separate industries, it seems desirable to consider briefly some of the broad general forces which have been in operation to produce this relatively sudden and widespread substitution of conscious artificial control for the unconscious control of a *laissez-faire* system, and to indicate certain general aspects of this revolutionary development in industrial organisation; these should be kept in mind when studying the stories of particular industries, and their particular control schemes, or else we may run the risk of missing the wood for the trees. There are, for instance, a good many people who think that, with the isolated exception of the British rubber restriction scheme of 1922, artificial control schemes in the primary industries are a product of the present world depression which began in 1930, and that this whole development in industrial organisation should be looked upon primarily as a means of combating acute general world trade depressions. This view is based on sheer ignorance of facts, and naturally the deduction is likely to be equally fallacious and misleading. Even before 1929 there had been experiments in artificial control, on a sufficiently large scale to affect world supplies and world prices, in wheat, sugar, coffee, rubber, petroleum, copper, lead and zinc: and by the middle of 1929 control schemes were being generally discussed in connection with cotton and tin. This is an important proportion of the world's primary products, though we must not forget the existence of wool, silk, flax and jute, tea, meat and dairy products, hides, and many other products of less importance, in which artificial control was not being seriously considered. But there is no room for misunderstanding as to the widespread existence of artificial control schemes before the world depression began, and of these schemes, that for rubber dates back to 1922, those for sugar and copper to 1926, while coffee was really almost continuously controlled from 1917, and there had been partial control of copper and tin during the post-war slump of 1920–21.

We shall therefore have to look farther back than 1929 for the general causes of the development of artificial control schemes in the primary industries. I mentioned above that, even before the war, the movement towards combines in manufacturing industry had developed to a stage where the monopolistic control of the output of national industries had become fairly widespread in the form either of trusts or cartels, and international agreements for the same purpose were by no means unknown. The combination of previously independent concerns, whether by complete amalgamation or agreement, had also proceeded some way in the mineral industries, especially perhaps in the great copper industry of the United States; while there had actually been partial control schemes in aluminium and zinc. But as I also said, the small-scale unit of most agricultural industries, and the consequent multiplicity of independent producers, made the prospects of effective combination to control output, prices or stocks remote, even on a national basis, while in such cases as wheat or sugar, there are many nations all over the world which make a substantial contribution to the volume of world trade in these products, quite apart from those which produce primarily for home consumption. Thus the possibility of achieving monopolistic control of even a part of the world market was insignificant in agricultural industries. But that is not to say that agriculturalists were wholly indifferent and completely unimpressed by the developments towards monopolistic combination in manufacturing. On the contrary it was rather that they regarded these developments with wistful and longing eyes, as do those who see a paradise beyond their reach: while mineral producers were equally desirous and much more hopeful, for their reach was considerably longer. Thus the developments of industrial organisation in manufacturing may be said to have pointed a course towards the same goal for the producers of primary products. The movement towards conscious control has been common throughout industry as a whole for the last fifty years or more, and the significance of this should not be missed.

But artificial control in the primary industries might have been delayed almost indefinitely if it had not been for the Great War. The Great War had two very different effects; it made artificial control appear more necessary and desirable, and, secondly, it made it appear far more practicable than previously. Artificial control became more necessary and desirable because of the tremendous dislocations of all kinds which the Great War brought about. In the first place, production was greatly diminished in some countries and enormously stimulated in others: for example, Russia and the Danubian countries ceased to export wheat, and Canada and some other countries greatly increased their production in order to make good the deficiency: the best sugar lands of Europe were sown with shells instead of beet-roots, and consequently Cuba planted vast tracts of virgin land with sugar cane to try to compensate matters. Secondly, some raw material industries found their pre-war markets closed to them. Brazil lost her large pre-war market for coffee in Germany: Lancashire was left with an insufficient labour force to utilise the same volume of American cotton, while rubber producers and tin miners in Malaya suffered through inability to get their production to the chief markets owing to the shortage of shipping. To a large extent these difficulties disappeared fairly rapidly after 1918, but in some cases they left their mark in the form of permanent changes in taste or customary expenditure, and in general they added to the war-time commotion. Again, these difficulties drove home to countries like Brazil and Malaya, whose national economic prosperity depends upon the export of one or two commodities, a lesson on the disadvantages of having all their eggs in one basket, a lesson which was repeated in these and other cases, such as Cuba and the West Indian Islands, during the post-war slump. Thirdly, the war taught several of the belligerent and some neutral countries the disadvantages of depending on distant lands for supplies of essential foodstuffs and raw materials in time of war, and made them determine to try and reduce this dependence by increased home or imperial production: in other words, it increased the tendency towards economic nationalism, and this of course created new difficulties for the exporting countries. Thus both importing and exporting countries increased each other's difficulties, the former striving to reduce their dependence on the latter for foodstuffs and raw materials, and the latter their dependence on the former for manufactured goods. And where exporting countries could do little, owing to the nature of their resources, either in the direction of developing other export industries or home manufacturing industries, their governments were driven to watch more closely the fortunes of the one or two industries upon which the government revenues and the general national prosperity depended, and to offer any assistance which lay within their power. Thus the Great War produced changes of many kinds, and a general state of instability, and it seemed more and more difficult to believe that equilibrium could be restored most effectively and most speedily by leaving economic forces to operate unchecked and without artificial encouragement: on the contrary, it seemed that only by direct intervention on the part of the leaders of industry and their governments could more stable conditions be re-established.

The second effect of the Great War was to make direct government intervention or artificial control appear much more practicable. In all the belligerent countries, and in many neutral countries, governments were forced to intervene much more definitely in economic affairs, to undertake themselves the production of munitions, to operate railways and shipping, to organise rationing schemes for foodstuffs and in some cases for raw materials,[1] and to become merchants on a scale undreamed of by private concerns.[2] Governments, in fact, not only did things which would previously have been considered an unwarrantable interference with business, but they did things which had hitherto been deemed virtually impossible for any single man or committee, owing to the practical difficulties of

[1] E.g. the Cotton Control Board in Great Britain.
[2] E.g. in wool through the British Australian Wool Realisation Association.

organisation and administration. It is true that these
things were sometimes done inefficiently and at great
cost, but they were done, and done better and more
cheaply as time went on and much valuable experience
was gained. The result was greatly to widen men's
ideas not only as to the possible role of governments
in economic affairs, but as to methods of industrial
organisation, and in particular as to the possibilities of
collective control over whole industries. And in this
respect the need of governments to deal with industries
as a whole led to a good deal of corporate organisation
in many manufacturing and mining industries, and
even to a certain amount of such organisation in some
agricultural industries. What governments could enforce upon an industry in the form of artificial control
of production, stocks, price or markets, could obviously
be done by the industry itself, provided it was organised
under the control of a dictator or a committee; the
potentialities of such organisations were thus increased
at the same time as the possibilities of their formation.

The war-time measures of artificial control undoubtedly led to a number of similar sorts of control
in the immediate post-war years. Thus the copper
producers of the United States had read, marked,
learned, and sufficiently digested the lessons of the war
years to form a pool of the surplus stocks, which were
rapidly accumulated during the post-war depression of
1920–21, in order to dispose of them gradually, as and
when the demand recovered: at the same time a more
or less effective and very drastic restriction of pro-

duction was enforced. The satisfactory experience of the British and Australian Governments in dealing with surplus stocks of wool which could not be brought to Europe during the war years owing to the scarcity of shipping, naturally helped to encourage the British Government in its efforts to persuade the Dutch Government to join in establishing, by the Bandoeng agreement of 1920, a pool for surplus tin stocks in the Middle East, similar to that which was established privately by the American copper producers. Again, it was the war-time difficulties of temporarily closed markets which led Brazil to renew her pre-war experiments in coffee control, and the success of this valorisation of 1917 led on to the policy of permanent control. Finally, it must be remembered that the voluntary rubber restriction scheme by British companies in Malaya during 1917 paved the way for the still wider voluntary scheme of 1920, and there is little doubt that without its war-time experience the British Government would hardly have dared to introduce compulsory government restriction when the voluntary scheme broke down, even if it had dreamed of doing so.

Many people regard the copper and tin pools of 1920–21 as mere legacies from the war period, to be classed along with the many controls during the actual war years, and without real significance for the developments in artificial control which emerged a few years later. I do not know how this view can be reconciled with the facts of the gradual and almost continuous evolution of artificial control in coffee and rubber, though I should be the first to admit that these copper and tin pools have marked "war control" characteristics, and differ in many obvious and important respects from the subsequent control·schemes in these or other industries. But it seems to me difficult, if not impossible, to deny that these pools were forerunners of the copper control scheme of 1926 and the tin control scheme of 1930, and, as such, first cousins to their contemporaries the rubber and coffee schemes, while all these four must own kinship to the war-time controls, albeit as a distinctive branch of the family tree, just as all the later controls must include both war and immediate post-war controls in their ancestry. In short, there is a definite and clear line of evolution, the denial of which seems to me to contravene all historical sense, and to obstruct a full understanding of the significance of the evolutionary process.

Further stress must however be laid on the participation of governments in these earlier control schemes. In the main, artificial control in manufacturing industry has been established without governmental aid, and simply by the voluntary efforts of the business men concerned: indeed, manufacturers as a rule have been careful to give governments no chance or cause to intervene. But as has already been said, in most agricultural industries, and also, though to a lesser extent, in mineral industries, the producers are too numerous, and too widespread in different quarters of the globe, to establish an effective corporate organisation without the aid of the governments concerned. Moreover, the technical problems of controlling supplies of raw materials are far more difficult and hazardous than is the case with most manufactured goods. It should also be borne in mind that the economic activities of a manufacturing nation are usually fairly diverse, and the government revenues and the general economic prosperity rarely depend on the fortunes of one or two industries. In many cases the reverse is true of countries which produce primary products, and therefore their governments are likely to be far more sympathetic to calls for assistance in organising or operating a control scheme, while they may even feel it to be their duty to the nation to take the initiative themselves and to impose a control scheme against the wishes of a large section of the industry concerned: such initiative was taken by the British Government on behalf of Malaya in respect of the rubber restriction scheme of 1922. Thus the evolution of conscious control in the primary industries is distinguished from the same evolution in manufacturing industries by the willingness of the producers to invoke government aid, and the readiness with which governments respond or even take the initiative. This attitude on the part of governments seems to me again clearly traceable to their needs and experiences during the Great War. If the attitude of governments had not changed, the development of artificial control in the primary industries would probably have remained a practical impossibility for a very long time.

Chronologically the next important attempt at control after the British rubber restriction scheme was the restriction of her sugar crops by Cuba beginning in 1926, and about the same time the Brazilian coffee control was finally established on what was intended to be a permanent basis; it has indeed been permanent, but not quite in the way intended! Copper control also came in 1926, and then, in 1928 and the first half of 1929, came the end of the British rubber restriction, the establishment of partial controls in lead, zinc, and petroleum, the influence exerted on wheat by the Canadian pools, and much talk of restriction for the tin industry, and for various agricultural products in the United States including cotton. Without going into greater detail, which will be found in the following chapters, it is clear that by 1928 restriction schemes were being freely hatched. The need for them seemed not to diminish, but to grow with increasing world prosperity, and I want to stress this point. No one can deny that the world was prospering in the years 1926–29. The consumption of all foodstuffs was increasing, though not in many cases at the pre-war rate of increase per head of population; the demand for most raw materials, however, was increasing by leaps and bounds. The world, and especially Europe, was in fact recovering from the effects of the Great War at a speed which few people anticipated. And yet the producers of many foodstuffs and raw materials were experiencing such difficulties, as the result of excessive supplies and falling prices, that they were induced to experiment with artificial control schemes as a means of lessening the existing strain, and preventing the increase of that strain which otherwise seemed inevitable. The following chapters will show that the circumstances of each industry differed very considerably, but in almost all cases it will be seen that fundamental difficulties arose from the existence of a total productive capacity so much in excess of what was required to meet the demand that the price could not be even mildly profitable to a substantial proportion of that capacity. Again, the precise causes of this excess of capacity differ very considerably from industry to industry, but, without wishing to prejudice the reader in advance, it may be of assistance to suggest that, in reading the stories of the different industries, he should give careful attention to the rapid advance in the technique of production, which has been a feature in so many cases. Until the reader has digested the stories of particular industries, it would be both improper, and useless, for me to try and assess the quantitative significance of this advance in productive technique, or to consider in what ways such technical progress may create conditions of excess capacity. Further consideration of these matters is therefore deferred to the concluding chapters. I have given this hint here, simply in order to try and help the reader to form ideas as to the common characteristics of the wood, while he is examining the peculiarities of its component trees; and I must add that technical progress is in any case only one of these common characteristics, and that I am far from suggesting that in itself it offers a complete explanation.

With the onset of the world trade depression in the autumn of 1929, the whole situation changes. After the Wall Street crash, merchants and manufacturers, especially those in the United States, virtually stopped buying for a time, and the result was a fall in the prices of most primary products as drastic as it was sudden. This caused the virtual breakdown of almost all the existing control schemes, and for a short time in the spring of 1930 it looked as if the individualist *laissez-faire* system would be restored. Though as the first shock passed, merchants and manufacturers, having used up their stocks, began buying again for immediate requirements, it was soon evident that the volume of these immediate requirements was very much below that of 1929, and rapidly shrinking every day. Where there had been little or no surplus capacity in 1929, that problem now appeared, and where it had already been present in 1929, the situation rapidly became desperate. In these latter industries, it seemed clear that if artificial control had been previously desirable and necessary, it was obviously more than ever desirable and necessary now, while several of the former industries became converted to its merits. Thus old schemes were revived, revised and extended, and new schemes were set on foot. Practical difficulties of organisation were in some cases responsible for considerable delay in establishing or re-establishing control schemes, but one followed another, until all those industries which had experimented with artificial control before 1929 had renewed these experiments, usually on an even greater scale, and new control schemes had been established in cotton, tin and tea, to mention only the more important products. Wool, flax, jute, meat and dairy products alone remain substantially free from any general control scheme. Thus artificial control has been applied almost as a panacea for the troubles of the last few years, irrespective of the very different circumstances of different industries: in particular no distinction seems to have been drawn between industries which were "in trouble" before the world trade depression began, and those whose troubles have been due solely to the depression and the resulting fall in demand; equally, no distinction seems to have been drawn between a fall in demand due to reduced purchasing power, and one due to decreased dependence of customers on the world market, owing to increased home production under the protection of tariffs or subsidies. Here again I throw out a hint to the reader that common sense provides a *prima-facie* case in favour of paying attention to such distinctions.

This widespread adoption of artificial control since 1930 is perhaps all the more extraordinary because the record of control schemes up to that date cannot be said to have provided much encouragement. The British rubber restriction scheme of 1922 had come to an inglorious end in 1928; Cuba had in the same year given up, in utter disgust and despair, the drastic restriction schemes which she had been operating and perfecting for four years; the copper control of 1926, and Brazil's coffee valorisation were riding for obvious and certain falls long before the Wall Street crash loomed up: the other controls of the period had hardly got into their stride, and so provided no evidence either for or against. But all this dismal history did not damp the faith of those who had experienced it, nor prejudice the onlookers. The general strength óf the movement towards artificial control is clearly immense; and it has recently been increased by the operations of certain controls, notably the tin and rubber schemes, which in the last year or two have successfully raised prices, and restored a measure of reasonable prosperity to the industries concerned, while in other industries it is fairly clear that, though not by any means as successful, conditions would have been very much worse than they actually have been, if there had been no attempt at artificial control. Due weight must be paid to such facts, but it is nevertheless true that results in the long period may be very different from those in the short period. A patient may feel much better after a good dose of brandy, but his ultimate chances of recovery may be lessened: on the other hand, such a dose at the right time may enable him to turn the corner, and recover more speedily, and even perhaps therefore more completely. This moral in terms of sick men may legitimately be applied to sick industries, and again without wishing to prejudice the reader in advance of a sufficient knowledge of the facts, I would ask him to be careful in formulating judgments exclusively on the basis of immediate results, especially when the long-run results are what really matter. We do not yet know enough about the way in which artificial control schemes work out in the long run: at best we can only formulate for ourselves an interim report on the whole subject: but in making it we must try and analyse the past and the present, in order that we may be better able to look a little way into the future. This analysis is no easy task, but we had certainly better not attempt it until we know more of the facts of the past and the present. It is hoped that the following chapters on particular industries may go some way towards supplying this knowledge, and then we can return to a general study of this new and most vitally important development in industrial organisation with a view to analysing its merits and demerits, and so forming the best judgment possible for our practical guidance in these matters.

Chapter II

CONTROL SCHEMES IN COFFEE

FOR nearly two whole years well over one million people in Brazil started working almost with the dawn each day, and worked all day for six months of each year in really sweltering heat, and for the other six months in a sun as hot as in the hotter summers in England. They worked at weeding, pruning and generally looking after about 2000 million coffee trees. Towards the end of each year, with much labour, they gathered an average crop. They then prepared these crops for the market by a long series of operations, after which the coffee was carried by mules or by lorries over very rough roads anything from 5 to 20 miles to the nearest railway station, from which it was dispatched on a journey of anything from fifty to two hundred miles. At the end of that journey, it was thrown into enormous heaps, and with the aid of petrol these heaps were set alight, and the fires kept going until the last coffee bean had been completely and utterly destroyed. Two whole years' work gone up in smoke! Enough coffee to have supplied the whole world for nearly a year and a half!

This story is not strictly accurate, but it is only untrue in the sense that a part of each of a series of crops has been burnt instead of two whole crops; the net result has been the same as in the story. During the last four years Brazil has burnt a quantity of coffee equal to two good average crops. Everyone has heard of this burning of coffee in Brazil, but perhaps some people have not appreciated the gigantic scale on which it has been done, nor perhaps thought of the tremendous expenditure of labour and capital involved in the production of all the coffee which has been burnt. No matter how one looks at the thing, it is clearly an appalling state of affairs—worse, in a way, than anything which has happened in connection with other commodities—and I therefore propose to begin our studies of particular control schemes with coffee, and to try to explain why sheer destruction of part of their coffee crops was thought by the Brazilians to be the only way of escape from their difficulties.

Brazil produces about 60 per cent. of the world's supply of coffee even to-day, and ten years ago the proportion was nearly 70 per cent. The balance comes, firstly, from a group of countries on either side of the Panama Canal, notably Colombia, Venezuela, Costa Rica, Honduras, Salvador and Guatemala; secondly, from the Dutch East Indies; thirdly, from some of the West Indian Islands, notably Haiti; while, lastly, what is in comparison a small supply has for a long time come from the state of Mysore in India, and in recent years from Central Africa, that is, from Kenya, Tanganyika and the Belgian Congo. Now, the production of these other countries, the so-called "mild" coffee countries, does not vary much from year to year, whereas Brazil's crop varies enormously owing to the weather and other conditions. Moreover, these "mild" coffees are of much better average quality than Brazilian coffee, and are therefore all bought in preference to Brazilian coffee. Consequently the adjustment of production and consumption for the world as a whole in any year, and the general price level of coffee, really depends upon the Brazilian crop. And that is why the story of coffee is so largely the story of Brazilian coffee, and why it was in Brazil, and not in other coffee-producing countries, that the difficulties of excessive production became so acute as to necessitate such terrible waste and destruction.

Since Brazil is a part of the world which is not very well known to Englishmen, a few general remarks about the country may not be amiss. The area of Brazil is roughly the size of Europe: it is a great deal bigger than it looks on some maps! From the economic point of view, the country may be divided into a number of zones, mainly owing to the variations in the climate over such a huge territory. There is, first of all, the Amazon valley where the climate is purely tropical. It used to be the source of almost the whole of the world's rubber supplies, but with the development of the rubber industry in the East, the Amazon valley production has greatly declined, and is now relatively unimportant. The second zone is the northern coastal provinces: here again the climate is tropical, and the chief products are sugar and cocoa. Thirdly come the three middle coastal provinces of St Paulo, Rio and Minas Geraes. This is the most heavily populated, the most highly de-

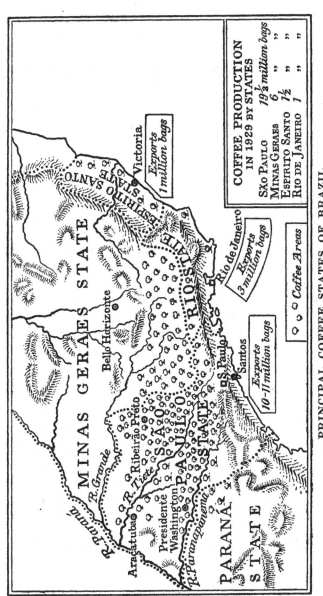

COFFEE PRODUCTION
IN 1929 BY STATES

SÃO PAULO	19½ million bags
MINAS GERAES	6 ,, ,,
ESPIRITO SANTO	1½ ,, ,,
RIO DE JANEIRO	1 ,, ,,

Victoria.

Exports
1 million bags

ESPIRITO SANTO
STATE

MINAS GERAES STATE

Bello Horizonte

RIO STATE

Rio de Janeiro

Exports
3 million bags

Coffee Areas

R. Grande

R. Tieté

Ribeirão Preto

SÃO
PAULO
STATE

S. Paulo

Santos

Exports
10–11 million bags

Araçatuba

Presidente
Washington

PARANÁ
STATE

R. Paranapanema

R. Paraná

PRINCIPAL COFFEE STATES OF BRAZIL

veloped, and the most wealthy part of Brazil, because this is the coffee zone: it is this bit of Brazil which is shown in the map on p. 25. Fourthly, there are the southern states with a climate ranging from sub-tropical to temperate: some coffee is grown in the north of this zone—in Parana—but most of it is cereal and general farming land. Then there is the inland western fringe of all these zones, of which parts have been developed as cattle country, and finally, still further to the west, there is the virtually unknown and unexplored forest area.

Brazil was, of course, colonised by the Portuguese, the native Indians being gradually driven westwards into the interior: Portuguese is thus the language, not Spanish as so many people think. The first big immigration was the compulsory transference of negro slaves from Africa to the northern coastal provinces to work the sugar plantations. Voluntary immigration began later, and has been on a very large scale since about 1870. It has mainly consisted of southern Europeans who were drawn to the middle zone of Brazil by the rapid development of the coffee industry. The coffee planters as a whole have always preferred white labour, and the labour on the coffee plantations is mainly of European stock. The total population of Brazil is now over forty millions, but this is nothing in view of the size of the country, especially as a large proportion of the total is located in the coffee zone.

As has been said, it is the middle coastal zone which is the coffee country, and more than two-thirds of

Brazil's coffee crop is grown in the State of St Paulo. The physical features of this bit of country are that along the coast there lies a mountain plateau, three or four thousand feet high and some ten miles broad. This plateau is precipitous on the coastal side, but on the other side the country rolls away gradually lower and lower right across to the great Parana river. One wants to think of the coffee country as a gently undulating plain, gradually getting lower and lower as one goes west. As regards the climate, there is a wet season roughly from November to March, and this is also the hottest season. The winter, from April to October, is dry, and usually there is a prolonged period of hot sunny days and fairly cool nights. General and serious frost occurs only at intervals of ten to twenty years: even these serious frosts are what we should call very slight, but the coffee tree is damaged by even an hour or two of a temperature only two or three degrees below freezing. A more frequent, though less serious, source of damage is the cold winds which sweep up from the south.

Now the city of St Paulo is situated more or less in the middle of the mountain plateau, and the country has been developed from the mountains westwards, so that the farther west or north-west one goes from St Paulo, the less developed the country becomes; there are still large areas of undeveloped land before the Parana River is reached. As the result of the gradual penetration and development of the country westwards during the last thirty or forty years, St Paulo is the centre of a great arc of a circle, on the circumference of which the conditions are those of pioneering and frontier developments. St Paulo itself, however, is a highly developed, modern European, or American city of over a million people, with fine buildings, splendid houses, shops and banks; this also applies in some degree to the smaller towns within one hundred miles. But as one travels west, the roads get worse, the railways become fewer and smaller, and the general economic development less and less.

So much by way of a general description of Brazil and the principal coffee states. Now a word or two about the cultivation of coffee trees. The coffee tree would be more accurately described as a large thick bush[1] which reaches its prime in about twelve years, and on good land it will be perhaps 8–15 feet high, with a diameter of about 12 feet. The trees will bear a reasonable crop in four to five years, though they do not reach their maximum yield until they are fully grown, that is in ten to twelve years. After the trees are twenty years old, their size and foliage gradually diminish, and so therefore does the yield of berries. But even in its prime in a good year, a coffee tree will only yield about $2\frac{1}{2}$ lb. of coffee, and so an enormous number of trees are required to produce the 15–20 million bags, each weighing 132 lb., which constitute an average crop in recent years. The trees are raised from seed, and the main business of cultivation is to keep down the weeds which would otherwise check the growth of the trees, and later, when the tree bears, the

[1] See illustration facing this page.

Picking coffee in Brazil

General view of a coffee estate

Drying coffee berries on the terraces

ground beneath it must be made absolutely clean and firm, because the method of picking in Brazil is simply to strip the branches by running the hand down them, allowing the berries to fall on to the ground. Then they are raked up, and put through a sieve to remove any dust, leaves or bits of stick, etc. Broadly speaking one man and his family can look after 4000 trees. Thus the cultivation of coffee lends itself to operations on a large scale. In Brazil there are twenty-one estates with over a million trees, but these very large estates are quite exceptional. There are a fair number with 50,000 to 200,000 trees, but the most common size is between 10,000 and 50,000 trees. On the other hand, there are over 13,000 estates with less than 5000 trees, so that a substantial part of the industry is in the hands of what may be called peasant proprietors, because such small estates will be worked by the owner and his family, with a little hired labour for the picking of the crop. A very few of the bigger estates are owned by British companies; all the rest are owned by Brazilians, and even the largest are still family concerns, and are not organised in joint stock company form.

In the centre of the estate[1] will be the factory for the preparation of the coffee berries as they come from the tree. The fruit of the coffee tree is like a very small cherry, only the stone is in two halves, and it is these two halves which are the coffee beans. The berries are usually dried in the sun on enormous terraces,[2] where

---

[1] See upper illustration facing this page.
[2] See lower illustration facing this page.

great heaps of them are constantly turned over, either by hand, or by mules which drag boards behind them. As it dries, the berry splits and releases the two beans, which must then be milled by machinery in order to remove a sort of parchment skin with which they are covered. Finally the beans are graded, put into sacks and taken either by mule cart, or in these days more often by lorry, to the railway station, whence the coffee is dispatched to the ports. Santos is the port and market for almost the whole of the production of the State of St Paulo: Rio de Janeiro for the States of Rio and of Minas Geraes. At Santos and Rio the coffee is sold to exporters, and shipped to the United States, Europe and elsewhere.

It was said above that the Brazilian crop varies greatly from year to year owing to the weather, but this is only half the story. Good weather for the coffee tree means abundant rain during the Brazilian summer —that is our winter—and during the Brazilian winter sufficient sunshine and not too low a temperature. Suppose then that the weather is very good, and a bumper crop results. The bearing of this bumper crop greatly exhausts the vitality of the trees, and even if the good weather continues, the next crop will almost certainly be much below normal. The bearing of this light crop rests the tree, but normally it is not in a condition to bear a second bumper crop for at least three or four years. After that, the bumper crop may come any time, depending simply upon the weather. Hence there is a fairly regular normal cycle of bumper crops followed by two or three short crops and then more or less average crops, unless and until the weather produces another bumper crop. Broadly speaking the bumper crop is double the short crop.

Now this crop cycle is a great trouble from the point of view of prices. The demand for coffee does not vary very much, even though the price may vary a great deal. In the great coffee-drinking countries like the United States and on the European continent, people do not consume much more coffee when it is cheap, any more than people in England consume much more tea when it is cheap. Similarly, they do not consume much less when coffee is dear. Consequently, even though the price of a bumper crop was very much reduced, not much more than usual would actually be consumed. The surplus over normal consumption has to be purchased by merchants and stored until it is wanted to make up the deficiency of the short crop, and this storage is perfectly feasible because coffee does not deteriorate for several years. In bumper-crop years, therefore, the planters used to get a very low price for their coffee. They had to sell practically the whole of their crop in order to get cash to meet the abnormally high *total* cost of harvesting a bumper crop. The merchant then stored the surplus until the next year, and therefore in the short-crop year the amount of coffee on offer in the market might not be much less than the normal consumption, with the result that the price in the short-crop year would not be much above normal, even though the costs *per bag* of producing that short crop were much greater than the costs *per bag* of producing a normal crop. The planter felt that the merchant had it both ways, not realising, perhaps, the heavy costs of storing and financing the unwanted surplus, and forgetting that competition between merchants must prevent their making continuously excessive profits. The planter might see the coffee which he had sold to a merchant one year, sold by that merchant, perhaps only twelve to eighteen months later, at a price half as high again or more. And he felt that if a bumper crop meant low prices, a short crop ought to mean high prices. The planter became convinced that if only some scheme could be evolved to hold back the surplus from the market in the bumper year, then the price in the bumper year would not be so disastrously low, and subsequently they would get the fat profits which the merchants seemed to be making. The fact that most of the big merchant firms are foreign companies—chiefly British, American and German—also perhaps added to the planters' discontent. Moreover, these views found support from the politicians in Brazil though on quite different grounds. Coffee forms no less than 70 per cent. of the total value of Brazil's exports, and if the value of the exports of coffee falls, the trade balance of Brazil is disturbed, and the foreign exchanges turn against her. Moreover, from taxation and other general political points of view, it must be realised that coffee is the hub of the whole economic life of the most important part of the country. If the coffee planters are prosperous and have plenty of money to pay good wages, everyone is prosperous, and trade generally thrives. If the coffee industry is depressed, the whole economic life of the country is depressed.

Thinking along these lines, the planters and the Government of the State of St Paulo were led to experiment with what are usually called Valorisation Schemes. I do not propose to say anything about the early experiments in pre-war years and during the war. Whether these schemes really brought any *net* benefit to the planters or the country is doubtful. Perhaps on the whole there was a small net benefit, but what matters is that both the Government and the planters were quite certain that there was a great benefit. Consequently, in 1923 a permanent scheme of control was started, whereby the price was to be maintained at what was considered a reasonably profitable level for a normal crop, and if in any year the whole crop could not be sold at this price, the surplus was to be stored until there was a corresponding deficiency. Under the scheme, special state warehouses were established in the interior, to which the planters had to dispatch all their coffee. From these warehouses coffee was sent to the market at Santos as it could be absorbed. If the price went up, more coffee was released from the warehouses until the price fell again to the correct figure: if the price went down, less was released until it rose again.

That part of the scheme is relatively simple to describe. But the vital part was the financial arrangements, and those were rather more complicated. For, of course, the planters could not be expected to wait without payment until their coffee was sold, since, on the basis of past experience of crop cycles, that might well be two or three years. In the normal way the banks advanced money to the big merchant firms on the security of the coffee which they had bought from the planters and were holding in their regular warehouses at Santos or Rio; and the merchants were then able to pay the planters. But it was another thing for the banks to advance money direct to the planters far away up-country, and on the security of coffee deposited in state warehouses from which it could not be got at the will of the banker. The banks, therefore, might not be willing to finance the planter under the valorisation scheme. And so a special state bank was created on the strength of a large loan obtained in London, and any planter could get an advance against the receipt given him for his coffee by the state warehouses from this state bank, even if the ordinary banks were unwilling to give it him. So long, therefore, as this bank had funds in hand wherewith to advance money to the planters, coffee could be withheld from sale for an indefinite period, for the bank would advance 70–80 per cent. of the current value of his crop to the planter, and this would amply cover his cash expenses of production. When his coffee was released and sold, the planter paid back the advance he had obtained, and any balance was his final profit.

That is the bare outline of the machinery of the valorisation scheme. All went well for the first few years, and the machinery was gradually perfected. In the years 1923–26 the task of the Coffee Institute (which was the title of the department which administered the scheme) was, indeed, easy, because, though there was a large crop in 1923, over the four years as a whole the supply of coffee was barely equal to the demand. It may in fact be doubted whether the control really made much difference over this period as a whole, though it certainly smoothed out price fluctuations. But then in 1927 came the test. That crop totalled 26 million bags as against an average demand of 14 to 15 million bags. But all went well. Further loans were raised wherewith to pay advances to the planters; the surplus was held back in the state warehouses; and though the price declined for a time, it was raised again, and maintained more firmly than ever at the desired figure. According to all precedents everything should have been well. For this huge bumper crop should have been followed by several short crops, owing to the exhaustion of the trees. The 1928 crop was indeed a short one—under 11 million bags—but then, to the amazement and horror of the Brazilians, the flowering of the 1929 crop was very heavy, promising a second bumper crop, which eventually proved to be no less than 29 million bags. This meant that a further 14–15 million bags would have to be stored in addition to the 10 million still in store from the first bumper crop: moreover advances would have to be made to the planters on this additional 14–15 million bags. The Coffee Institute went on bluffing that all was well, hoping to get still more loans from abroad, or special credits from the Bank of Brazil. But the Wall Street storm was now brewing in New York, and nothing could, therefore, be got from abroad, while the Federal Government would not allow the printing of paper money at home. Eventually, having come to the end of its finances, the Institute had to stop making advances, prices fell precipitously, and the whole scheme crashed down, much to the surprise of the world in general, for the Institute's bluff had been successfully swallowed.

Since the crash of October 1929, the story of coffee is the story of Brazil's attempts to liquidate the enormous stocks which had now piled up, and to re-establish some sort of equilibrium between production and consumption. But before I go on to this part of the story, I want to try and describe quite shortly the effects of the valorisation scheme on the coffee planters, and on Brazil generally, up to the time of the crash. The price which the Coffee Institute tried to maintain was deliberately fixed at a level which, it was calculated, would leave a reasonable profit in a normal crop year to the old estates with their relatively high costs. Now that means that the majority of estates could make more than normal profits on a normal crop, because their costs of production would be lower than those of the old estates. But that is not all. A large part of the costs of growing coffee consists of the costs of weeding and of the upkeep of the plantation generally, and above all of the interest on the original outlay of capital involved in planting out the estate, and maintaining it for four or five years until the trees reach bearing, during which time, of course, there is no return. Now the costs of current upkeep do not vary much with the size of the crop, and the interest charge not at all, and, together with other similar items, these fixed costs amount to between 70 and 80 per cent. of the total costs of a normal crop. Thus only 20–30 per cent. of the total costs vary with the size of the crop. Therefore a very large crop means a *total* cost greater than normal, but a cost *per bag of coffee produced* very much less than normal.

Now when the planters delivered the bumper crop of 1927 to the state warehouses—that is, the first bumper crop—they received a cash advance amounting to about 80 per cent. of the current market price, and since that price was designed to be profitable on a *normal* crop, this advance was considerably more than the costs per bag of this bumper crop. The planters, as a body, in fact found themselves with more money in their pockets than they had ever known before, and a period of great prosperity began for Brazil as a whole, and for St Paulo in particular. The prosperity of the planters communicated itself to their employees in the form of higher wages, and this meant a greater demand by the wage earners for manufactured goods, which benefited the manufacturing industries of St Paulo, as well as the merchants and the shop-keepers. The larger planters spent as much as they could on expensive town houses in St Paulo city, on trips to Europe and so on, but even so, they hardly knew how to spend it all. Some of the balance was invested in the establishment of new manufacturing enterprises, but of course the natural line of investment was to enlarge their coffee plantations, or to create new ones. Even before 1927 a lot of new planting had been going on in the interior, but from 1927 onwards the amount of new planting was enormous, since now there was ample money available in the country for this purpose. These new plantations had nothing to do with the appearance of the second bumper crop of 1929 so soon after that of 1927, because the new trees were not, of course, in bearing by 1929. But this new planting did mean that, from say 1932 onwards, the size of the normal crop would rapidly increase, and therefore, as well as the problem of enormous surplus stocks, there was the prospect of greatly increased crops within the next two or three years: in other words, the prospect of continually increasing excessive capacity, since consumption could not be expected to expand sufficiently even if there had been no world depression.

All this prosperity came to a most abrupt end with the crash in October 1929. By the end of that year coffee was selling at less than the advance which the planters had received for it: in other words, even when their coffee was released and sold, the planters found themselves still in debt to the banks, and most of them had no means of paying off such debts. The result in St Paulo was like the effect of frost on a coffee plantation. Overnight, healthy glossy green foliage and luxuriant growth—the next morning, a sea of brown withered branches. Planters who had been living in St Paulo city hurriedly went back to their plantations because there, for a time, all that they would need to buy was such food as could not be raised on the plantation. It is said that by the end of the year there were 100,000 high-class houses in St Paulo city for sale! The dealers and middlemen at Santos were similarly affected, and general trade became completely stagnant. The workers on the plantations were paid what was due to them for the crop just finished, but wages for the new season were reduced to a half, or even a quarter, of what they had been. For a time, many workers tried to obtain better terms by travelling to other districts, but they soon found that such better terms were not to be obtained, and that the best thing that they could do was to accept the new terms, since employment did at least mean a roof over their heads, and a patch of ground on which they could raise a considerable part of their food.

Let us now return to the course of events after the crash. If any sort of control was to be maintained over the amount of coffee offered for sale in the market, and therefore over the price of coffee, it was essential for the St Paulo Government to obtain money wherewith to make advances to the planters. The Federal President refused to allow any additional issue of paper money for this purpose, and therefore all hopes were concentrated on the possibility of obtaining further loans from abroad. Eventually, in April 1930, arrange-

ments were made for the great Coffee Realisation Loan
of £20,000,000. European and New York bankers
arranged to issue this loan on the security of a large
part of the stocks of coffee stored in the state warehouses. So much of these stocks were to be sold each
year, the exact amount depending on the estimated
size of the next two crops, and the proceeds of these
sales were to repay the loan within ten years. Meantime, the interest was to be provided from a special
tax on all coffee entering Santos. Thus the scheme
provided St Paulo with sufficient money to continue
the payment of advances to the planters, and therefore
to continue the general regulation of supplies, while at
the same time the surplus stocks were to be gradually
put on the market in amounts which, it was hoped,
would not result in unduly low prices. It was fondly
hoped that the whole problem had now been finally
solved, and that within a year or two all would be
going comparatively smoothly.

But such hopes were soon proved to be illusions.
The scheme was hardly started when a new complication arose, for in the summer of 1930, the Federal
Government was overthrown, and in the new Government, the State of St Paulo, and therefore the coffee
interests, had a much smaller representation. But the
new Federal Government could not, of course, neglect
the coffee problem, and one of its first acts was to take
over all the existing surplus stocks from the governments of St Paulo and other States. The handling of
the coffee problem thus passed completely and officially

into the hands of the Federal Government. And this was inevitable because the coffee problem was fundamentally linked with the other great problem which the new Federal Government had to face, namely, the problem of Brazil's foreign exchanges, and the fall in the value of the *milreis*, the Brazilian unit of currency. This had now become most serious. For though imports had been greatly reduced, the fall in the value of coffee had created an even greater reduction in the value of exports. If the price of coffee, and therefore the value of coffee exports, declined any further, the foreign exchanges were in imminent danger of collapse. It was, therefore, absolutely essential to try to prevent the price of coffee falling further, for it was certain that, unless something was done, the price would fall further, and a long way further, despite the Realisation Loan scheme. That scheme covered only the stocks in St Paulo on July 1st, 1930, and it had been estimated, three months before that date when the loan contract was made, that these stocks would amount to 16·5 million bags. This eventually proved to be too low an estimate by as much as 5 million bags. In addition, the scheme had not attempted to cover the considerable surplus stocks in other States, and so, in all, there were 7–8 million bags of surplus stocks over and above the 16·5 million bags covered by the Realisation Loan; these uncovered stocks would inevitably continue to exercise a very depressing influence on the price in the immediate future. And the outlook for the more distant future was equally bad, for as well as the problem of the existing surplus stocks, there was the problem of the future surpluses which would inevitably appear unless and until Brazil's capacity for production, on the basis of a normal crop yield, was brought into line with the world's demand for her coffee. With the world depression, there was little prospect of any considerable increase in the consumption of Brazilian coffee beyond the current rate of 15–16 million bags, and, on the other hand, there was the certainty that the future scale of normal crops would be much greater than this, in view of the enormous amount of new planting which had taken place between 1926 and 1929. In any case, the flowering in the early autumn of 1930 had given promise of another abnormally large crop in 1931. Something drastic had got to be done unless the whole economic and financial life of Brazil was to be drowned in the flood of unwanted coffee.

It may be thought that the obvious remedy in these circumstances was to introduce some form of crop restriction scheme, that is, to leave a certain percentage of the trees in each plantation unpicked. But crop restriction is simply not practical politics in the case of coffee. Unless each planter was supplied with sentries to keep watch throughout the picking season over that section of his plantation which was to remain unpicked, it is certain that someone else, if not indeed his own labourers, would pick those trees. The crop must therefore be picked, and the only possible form of crop restriction is to destroy a part of the crop after it has been harvested. But again, it is not practical politics to institute a scheme for destruction on each plantation. Such a scheme would require an army of inspectors, and even if their integrity could be guaranteed, it is certain that, in one way or another, a large proportion of the condemned coffee would never get destroyed. For these reasons, destruction to be effective would have to be carried out at a few big centres, where the matter could be properly supervised. Effective crop restriction, therefore, meant not only that the coffee must be grown and picked, but also transported a large part of the way to the market. But despite these expensive difficulties, the new Federal Government decided that destruction was the only remedy. Its first proposal was that each planter should hand over 20 per cent. of his crop for destruction. Considering the cost of this tax in kind to the planters, it is not surprising that a general outcry was raised, and that the scheme had to be given up after two or three weeks. Eventually in April 1931, it was decided to impose an export tax of 10s. a bag, payable by the exporter, the proceeds of which were to be used to buy up lower grade coffee and burn it; it was expected that at least five to six million bags a year could be dealt with in this way.

Thus it came about that Brazil had recourse to destruction as the only means of preventing the otherwise inevitable further large decline in the price of coffee, and the complete economic collapse of the whole country which that would have brought about. It may be argued that, after the crash of 1929, no further artificial control in any form should have been attempted, that the price of coffee should have been allowed to fall unhindered, and that in due course the very low prices would have brought about the abandonment of sufficient acreage to bring the supply into line again with the demand. But those who support such an application of *laissez-faire* doctrine should remember that this would have involved not only disaster to the coffee industry, but—in short—disaster to Brazil, for the whole national economic and financial structure of Brazil depends upon the coffee industry. Even so, it may admittedly be argued that this would have been the quickest and best way out of the difficulties with which Brazil was faced: in other words, that a general smash-up of the existing economic structure would have made possible a rapid rebuilding of a new and better structure, and that if things had been allowed to take their course, the economic condition of Brazil would have been better to-day, and still better in the near future, than it actually is or seems likely to be. There can in the nature of things be no definite answer to such arguments. But one may observe that it is not in human nature to submit to ruin without a struggle, and that no government or people can be expected to sit still and allow ruin to overtake them, on the chance that this will lead to a greater welfare for the next generation. It seems to me that in Brazil's case the doctrine of strict *laissez-faire*, whatever its merits, was simply not practical politics. The case for the policy of destruction is summarised, with only slight exaggeration, in the remark of a high official in the Brazilian

Government: "It is better to destroy coffee than to destroy human lives."

But a little more light can be thrown upon this problem if we finish the story. The policy of destruction began in April 1931, and it should also have been said that it was accompanied by a prohibition of new planting. At the end of that year, the export tax was raised to 15s., but the special tax guaranteeing the interest on the Realisation Loan was rescinded: so that this change did not really make much difference. A much more important change was the decision to purchase and destroy no less than 12 million bags during 1932, i.e. double the previous rate, the extra finance required for this being obtained by means of a large credit from the Bank of Brazil. These measures were taken in view of the abnormally large crop in 1931 which was now coming to the markets. This crop eventually proved to be about 27 million bags, not quite so big as that of 1929, but at least 11 million bags greater than the current annual consumption.

The destruction scheme adequately dealt with the surplus of the 1931–32 crop, but of course this large crop prevented any appreciable reduction of the previously existing surplus. The 1932 crop was relatively small, though, even so, it was, at 16 million bags, about as great as the annual consumption. But the rate of destruction was kept up by further borrowing, and at last some reduction of the surplus stocks began. Then in 1933 came yet another bumper crop of roughly 30 million bags. Many people might have given up the struggle in despair, but not so the Brazilians. It was ordained that the planters must sell 40 per cent. of their crop to the Government for destruction, at a price which would just about cover the direct costs of production on an average estate. This so-called "sacrifice" quota more or less did the trick, and as the 1934 crop was relatively small the situation became much easier, and there has been even some rise in the price of coffee in terms of gold, while in terms of Brazil's currency it has been very much greater, owing to the depreciation of the *milreis*. Indeed, at the beginning of 1935 the statistical situation of coffee seemed extremely strong as, according to the Brazilian Government, there were not more than 3–4 million bags of surplus stocks over and above those still held under the Realisation Loan scheme—these still amount to about 11 million bags but their gradual liquidation is provided for, and they cannot be put on the market at a greater rate. Unfortunately it is now certain that this estimate of the surplus stocks was too low: the surplus is at least 6 million bags. Moreover, despite the great drought in St Paulo during 1934, the 1935–36 crop will probably exceed the requirements of consumption by 2 million bags, so that at the end of June 1936 the surplus will probably be at least 8 million bags, while the profuse flowering of the trees in September 1935 indicates the possibility of another bumper crop in 1936–37, though of course many things may happen before it is ready for picking.

Despite the destruction of over 35 million bags, the

present position and the future outlook for the Brazilian coffee industry still remains extremely dark. On the other hand, apart from the coffee industry, economic conditions in Brazil have greatly improved during the last two years. The manufacturing industries of St Paulo are very busy behind the shelter of high tariff walls and exchange restrictions, and in some districts profits on a greatly increased production of cotton have helped even coffee planters to balance their accounts, though last year's cotton crop was a failure owing to the ravages of an insect pest. Elsewhere farmers have been developing a profitable trade as fruit growers. Reports indicate that the development of new frontier areas has been resumed, and in general a certain measure of economic stability has, at least for the moment, been restored. Except for coffee, a feeling of optimism has undoubtedly replaced the black pessimism of two years ago, and, even as regards coffee, the policy of destruction is considered to have been justified up to a point. But such facts should not blind us to other facts. In the first place, we must not minimise the price which Brazil has had to pay for her experiments in the valorisation or artificial control of coffee. The planters are all head over ears in debt, and the conditions of many estates will require a considerable outlay before really efficient production can be resumed. For nearly four years the workers on the plantations were receiving a small nominal sum in cash as their wages, though recently there has been a substantial advance owing to the demand for labour for cotton growing. The whole economic life of the country has indeed been so violently dislocated that it will require several years before normal economic stability, let alone prosperity, can be restored. And there is a second point concerning which one must not allow the present relatively satisfactory position to blind one's judgment. What are the chances of a return to reasonable prosperity in the coffee industry? It is easy to see now where the valorisation scheme went wrong. The level at which the price was stabilised was too high, in the sense that it stimulated a great deal of new planting in other countries, and still more within Brazil itself. Moreover, as regards the latter, another crucial mistake was the unnecessarily large amount of the advances received by the planters on the bumper crop of 1927, for this supplied them with the capital for new planting and so enabled them to respond to the stimulus of relatively high prices. It is probably true, as I have said, that the appearance of the second bumper crop so soon after the first was largely the result of good weather, and the failure of the valorisation scheme was to that extent a matter of sheer bad luck. But, even if the usual sort of crop cycle had taken place, Brazil would have had to face the problem of the rapid expansion of production in the mild countries, and, worse still, the problem of a serious excess of capacity within Brazil: in other words, the valorisation scheme might not have crashed as early as 1929, but it was bound to fail within the next few years. And it is this excess capacity which is now the great obstacle: the difficulty of the accumulated surplus stocks has in part been solved, but the excess of capacity remains virtually as great as ever. There has, of course, been some decline in the production of the older, and therefore higher cost, estates owing to inferior cultivation, and some abandonment of the oldest and less profitable portions of estates. But against this must be set the huge number of healthy young trees in virgin soil, giving enormous and still increasing yields as they approach nearer to their prime. It seems pretty clear, on the basis of the last four years, that the normal crop of to-day is at least 20 million bags, whereas the demand is not more than 16 million bags. And at present prices, or even at prices substantially lower as they were a year or so ago, there is no prospect whatever of estates being abandoned on anything like the scale required. It looks as if Brazil will have to go on destroying the surplus of good crops for an indefinite period. Only two things seem likely to make this unnecessary. The first is the development of a demand for some other product which can be cultivated in the place of coffee. Oranges have already done this up to a point, but fruit growing cannot provide a remedy on the scale required. Probably cotton is the most hopeful alternative, and cotton is now being planted on an already very large and rapidly increasing scale, partly as a crop by itself, but mainly in between the rows of coffee trees. As chapter v will show, the world is not exactly short of cotton fields, but if it be true that Brazil can produce cotton at half the lowest price at which the United States is prepared to do so, there may here be a real way of escape for Brazil from its dependence on coffee and all the troubles and difficulties which that has entailed, even though it be at the expense of the American cotton belt. Cotton growing is one possibility: the other is the occurrence of a frost sufficiently severe and widespread to kill the surplus number of trees. That such a frost will happen again one day is tolerably certain, for the records of the last 150 years show that severe frosts occur at an average interval of about twenty years. The last such frost was in 1918. Admittedly such a frost would ruin the planters concerned, but it would unquestionably solve the problem of excess capacity in the coffee industry as nothing else will ever do. Such frosts usually take place in June, July or August. Will it be next year? That is a question to which many people would like to know the answer.

Chapter III

CONTROL SCHEMES IN WHEAT

EVERY country in the world is a consumer of wheat, while nearly every country outside the tropics produces wheat, and in the vast majority of countries either the consumption, or the production, or both, are at present directly affected by legislative control. Countries which on balance consume more than they produce, have enacted legislation both in respect of their home production and in respect of their wheat imports, and this has had a profound effect on the demand for the exports of those countries which produce more than they consume. But though, partly in consequence, the big exporters have also passed legislation with the object of improving their export trade by securing some control over the world market and so over the world price, such national legislation has, in general, met with little real success owing to the fact that even the large exporters are comparatively numerous, and hence no one of them is in a sufficiently commanding position; while the one and only international agreement has not been of much account. Artificial control schemes in some commodities have at least assumed the dimensions and importance of a tidal wave, but in wheat they have so far been little more than ripples on the surface, or at most local disturbances. But though, perhaps, the student of artificial control schemes will not learn much from the experiments in wheat control, which cannot be learned more clearly and decisively from the experiments in other commodities, yet the collective organisation which was built up by the wheat producers of one large exporting country, namely Canada, from 1923 onwards, and which was subsequently used as the machinery for attempts to control the world market and the world price, was in many ways unique, and deserves our close study; and in any case wheat is of such overwhelming importance amongst the primary products, that any attempts at control merit attention. But before we study these attempts we must briefly describe the conditions from which they evolved.

As everyone knows, wheat was falling in price, and wheat producers the world over were complaining of their inability to make adequate profits, for several years before the present world depression began. Now the troubles of wheat producers up to 1929 were in a fairly direct way due to the Great War, and it is essential to go back to the pre-war period in order to discover what the changes were which occurred during the war, and which caused so much trouble for such a long time afterwards. In the five years before the war, Western Europe was, as now, the biggest importer of wheat, and the biggest exporters were, in order, Russia with average annual exports of 19 million quarters, the United States with 13 million, Canada 12 million, and Argentina 10 million. Russia was thus by far the biggest exporter in the world, and in 1915 Russian exports suddenly and completely ceased. The magnitude of this war disturbance to the existing organisation of the world's wheat supplies can hardly be exaggerated, and it is not surprising that the re-establishment of a new equilibrium gave rise to correspondingly great difficulties. Stimulated by high prices, the acreage under wheat was rapidly increased in the United States and Canada, and eventually in Argentina and Australia. Consequently the war radically changed the relative importance of the world's wheat-exporting countries, and Europe came to draw its import requirements, first from Canada to the extent of 35–40 per cent. on the average, secondly from Argentina over 20 per cent., thirdly from the United States nearly 20 per cent. though her exports were slowly declining, and lastly from Australia rather more than 15 per cent. But, as so often happens when supply runs short and causes prices to rise far above normal, the increase in capacity was overdone, and soon after the war ended, not only was the loss of Russian exports made good, but also the decline in the wheat production of Europe: this had been directly caused by the war, as in the case of Germany, France and Italy, or as in the Danubian countries by the great social agrarian changes which arose out of the war. Actually the total world's supply in the five years 1920–24 was substantially greater than in the five years ending 1914.

Though the price level from 1920 to 1924 was considerably below the high level of the war years, wheat growing was still a very profitable undertaking on the new fertile lands which were continually being opened up in Canada, Australia and Argentina. Indeed, the tendency of prices to fall was to a considerable extent offset by the tendency of costs of production to fall, owing to the increasing opportunities for using machinery[1] which the petrol engine was providing, and owing to the application of science in the discovery of improved seed, manures, remedies for disease, and so on. In North America, Argentina and Australia this progress in productive technique could be exploited to the full, and so their wheat acreage and their yield per acre went on expanding year by year, despite the steady fall in price. But a still bigger increase in supplies was also coming from Europe, where under the stimulus of high tariffs production was not merely restored to the pre-war level, but raised considerably beyond that. Thus by about 1928 the world's available supplies of wheat were 15–20 per cent. greater than before the war, and though of course consumption had increased with the increase in world population, and probably also with the increase in the proportion of that population which consumes wheat, yet it was barely keeping pace with this very considerable increase in supplies, as is shown by the continuing fall in the price, and the tendency for stocks to increase, though until 1928 this increase was by no means serious.

In 1928, however, Nature decided to bring things to a head by providing very good crops almost all over

[1] E.g. the "combine-harvester" which thrashes as it reaps: an illustration faces page 64.

the world, and bumper crops in Canada and Argentina. In the autumn of 1928 the price fell considerably, and at the end of the year good milling wheat in Liverpool was fetching about 10s. a cwt. as compared with about 11s. 8d. the year before, having gradually fallen from an average of 15s. for the period 1920–24. But though the price fell in 1928, and continued to fall during the first half of 1929, it did not fall as much as might have been expected, because there was a firm general belief, especially in North America, that the persistent fall in wheat prices had gone on long enough, that a turn upwards was due, and that these large crops of 1928 would quickly be absorbed. Consequently, speculators readily came forward to buy the temporarily surplus supplies, hoping to profit by holding stocks until the price rose. Among these speculators was one very large and powerful one, the Canadian Wheat Pool, but further consideration of the Pool's activities can be postponed for the moment, since in the main it was only acting at this time in the same way, and under the same beliefs, as innumerable private individual speculators, though it may be true that some of these private speculators were buying in the belief that the Pool's activities would raise the price at any rate for a time. Looking back now, it seems hard to imagine how this belief in higher prices could have been so widely held, but one must remember that North America in general, led by the United States, was then convinced that general prosperity had come to stay, and to increase, and their whole economic outlook was viewed through rosy spectacles.

The Wall Street crash was accompanied by another good wheat crop in Europe, a somewhat sub-normal crop in the United States, and the smallest crop for years in Canada, while later the southern hemisphere crops of Argentina and Australia proved to be almost equally bad. Partly in consequence of this, and partly because the optimism of speculators in wheat was not wholly destroyed by the misfortunes of speculators in securities, the price of wheat was maintained until about February 1930. Then the crash came with a vengeance, and the average price of all wheat imported into Great Britain (which is probably the best indication of the general value of wheat in recent years) fell from well over 10s. per cwt. to 6s. in December 1930, and finally to 4s. 6d. in September 1931. From this there was some recovery, and the price during the 1931–32 season, beginning August 1st, averaged 5s. 9d. as compared with 6s. 1d. in 1930–31. In the 1932–33 season, the average was almost exactly the same as in 1931–32, but in 1933–34 it fell to 5s. 3d. Meantime, stocks had mounted to a peak by the end of the 1932–33 season, when they were equal to more than a year's import requirements, that is, rather more than double the normal level of convenience: in other words, surplus stocks amounted to at least six months' requirements. Then, in the summer of 1934, the weather decided to take a hand in the business, and the drought in North America, and in lesser degree in Europe, so reduced supplies as almost to wipe out surplus stocks except in Canada, and even these were much reduced. Prices naturally rose, and the average for 1934–35 was 5*s*. 10*d*. as compared with 5*s*. 3*d*. in the previous season.

This sketch of the course of prices and stocks is, however, rather meaningless unless it is related to the concurrent movements of production and consumption. Here the outstanding features of the first three seasons of world depression, that is, from July 1930 to July 1933, were, first, the steadiness of world consumption as a whole (though in part this was due to the diversion of much lower grade wheat from human to animal consumption); secondly, the steadiness of the acreage under wheat, and, on the average, of the resulting crops, in the three great exporting countries Canada, Argentina and Australia, though exports from the United States were dwindling; and, thirdly, the growth of production in the importing countries of Europe, which therefore steadily reduced their demands for imported wheat. In the season 1933–34, the first and third features were maintained, but supplies from the exporting countries were somewhat reduced as the result of the International Wheat Agreement of August 1933, and exports from the United States practically ceased, owing to the United States Government's reduction of acreage scheme. Thus, in very broad outline, the accumulation of stocks was due to the reduction in the demand by Western Europe for wheat imports consequent upon the growth of European production, and to the failure, on the one hand, of the exporting countries to reduce their exportable supplies, and, on the other hand, of consumption to increase, despite the tremendous fall in the price. The growth of European production was due partly to emergency agricultural relief measures, which by making it still profitable to grow wheat when nearly every alternative crop could only be grown at a loss, naturally resulted in farmers growing more—as has broadly been the case in Great Britain—but it has also been the last stages of a long process by which, ever since the war, the continental nations of Europe have been deliberately seeking to rebuild, and if possible to expand, their home production of essential foodstuffs, and to maintain their agricultural population. Even before 1929 this was only being achieved at increasing cost, because the peasant farmers of Europe, with their small-scale farms, could not take advantage of the progress of productive technique, which was so greatly reducing costs of production in the great exporting countries overseas: and when the world price of wheat crashed down in 1930, the continental nations were determined to preserve what was already in effect a costly investment. Hence the innumerable regulations and restrictions, tariffs and quotas, taxes and subsidies, to which wheat has been made subject in Western Europe. The combined result was successfully to maintain, and even increase, the internal price of wheat in consuming countries, despite the tremendous fall in the world price, and consequently consumption has not increased with that fall in price, because the price paid by the consumer has not in fact fallen. The exporting countries, therefore, found that any attempt which they made to stimulate demand by offering wheat at low prices, was immediately frustrated by their chief customers. There was no practical hope of increasing, or even maintaining, the demand for their wheat, and yet low prices did little to reduce their own production. The wheat farmer in Canada and Argentina virtually cannot grow anything in place of wheat: he must either grow wheat or give up farming, and he cannot save much of his cost by producing less wheat when prices fall. Certainly any large diversion to other crops can at best be a very gradual process, and in these years of depression there was nothing else for him to do but to hang on grimly, and grow wheat as long as it would bring him any return whatever over his minimum cash outlay in producing it.

Such is the general background against which we must now study the part played by artificial control schemes. There have been three main attempts at control: the first by the Canadian Wheat Pools beginning in 1928, the second by the United States Government beginning in 1930, and, thirdly, the International Wheat Agreement of 1933. But here it is not proposed to study the two last-named attempts in any detail, because the United States Government's operations in respect of wheat were of essentially the same character as its operations in cotton, which from the world point of view were much more important and will be described at length in chapter v, while the International Wheat Agreement, though interesting, was really of little importance. A very brief account will therefore be given in the next two paragraphs of these two attempts at artificial control, and then we shall proceed to a much fuller examination of the evolution and operations of the Canadian Pools.

In the summer of 1929 the United States Government established and financed the Federal Farm Relief Board to assist agriculture in general, and wheat and cotton in particular. This Board had hardly begun its task when the Wall Street crash began, and its first action took the form of making loans to the farmers at relatively cheap rates, in order to make it unnecessary for them to press their wheat on to a market in which prices were already falling, and liable to fall disastrously if the pressure of supplies were not reduced to a minimum. When, nevertheless, in February 1930 the price did fall disastrously, the Board, through its offspring the Grain Stabilisation Corporation, entered the Chicago market, and bought heavily in an attempt to stop the price-fall; and this was repeated in November 1930, and subsequently. By the early summer of 1931 the Corporation had come to the end of the resources which Congress was prepared to provide, and stopped buying, having accumulated no less than 250 million bushels, or nearly half the world's exportable stocks at that date. As a result, Chicago prices were maintained considerably above the level in other markets, and so far as the domestic price was concerned the American farmers clearly benefited. But of course this price disparity meant a big decline in exports which became still smaller in 1932. Indeed, one may broadly say that the United States ceased to be a wheat exporter from 1931 onwards, and her wheat problem became purely a domestic problem, so that she was no longer concerned with the international situation as it affected an exporter of wheat. Thus, during the 1932–33 season the Grain Stabilisation Corporation was able to maintain American prices at a premium above the world price, simply by continuing to withhold its stocks from the market, for the United States crop of 1932 was very far below normal owing to bad weather. The Corporation was however able to reduce its holdings very considerably by presenting wheat to the Red Cross Society for the benefit of the unemployed, by subsidising exports from the Pacific Coast and by sales to Asia on special credit terms. Then in the spring of 1933 President Roosevelt took office, and the whole policy was changed: the aim was no longer to be the control of prices by market operations, but the direct control of the acreage under wheat. Consequently the Federal Farm Board and the Grain Stabilisation Corporation were brought to an end, having cost the country millions of dollars. The Roosevelt policy for wheat was essentially similar to his policy for cotton, and may be summed up as reduction of acreage by compensation, the money being found by the imposition of a tax on flour. In 1934 it was only too successful, for in estimating the acreage necessary for home requirements the Secretary of Agriculture overlooked the vagaries of the weather, which, in the form of heat and drought, so reduced the crop that during the 1934–35 season the

United States, the world's second biggest exporter of wheat before the war, actually became an importer.

The International Wheat Agreement was concluded in August 1933. Following the failure of the World Economic Conference, the principal wheat exporting and importing countries engaged upon further discussions of what was now generally recognised to be as difficult a problem for the importers as for the exporters; the lower the price at which exporters were forced to sacrifice their wheat, the higher and the more costly were the tariffs, bounties, and restrictions which the importing countries found it necessary to impose, in order to protect their home producers. Under the agreement, the exporting countries agreed to limit their exports during the season 1933–34, and to reduce their acreage for the 1934 crop by 15 per cent. The importing countries in return promised not to increase their acreage under wheat, and to reduce their import duties if and when the world price had risen to an average of 63 gold cents for a continuous period of four months. The fundamental principle of the agreement was sound enough, and seemed to point the way towards a practical solution of what was, without such co-operation, a permanent impasse. But the method of acreage control was very difficult to enforce in practice, while acreage control does not mean any close control of production in particular years. Moreover early in 1934 Argentina, having harvested a bumper crop, deliberately exceeded her quota of exports, and though acreages for the 1934 crop were reduced, only in Australia was the reduction as much as 15 per cent. This, however, made little difference, for the weather of 1934 so reduced the yields of Canada and the United States that their crops were insufficient for the export of their full quotas. In view of the effects of the weather in raising the price, and more particularly in reducing surplus stocks during the 1934–35 season, coupled with the general attitude of Argentina—an attitude which was also largely shared by Australia—the agreement virtually became inoperative for the 1935 crop, though the International Wheat Committee, established under the agreement, has not been formally disbanded. The Wheat Agreement therefore cannot be said to have done more than slightly ease the pressure of exports during the 1933–34 season, and it might have done the same, but no more, during the 1934–35 season if the weather had not made its provisions unnecessary and inoperative. Nevertheless, as the International Committee formally affirmed last June, the wheat problem is by no means solved, and it may be that events will yet lead to fresh attempts at organised international control.

Having thus given some account of these attempts at control by the United States Government and through the Wheat Agreement, we can now turn back to the earlier experiments made by the Canadian Wheat Pools. First, however, some account must be given of the evolution of these organisations. For many years before the war the Canadian farmers had been discontented with the conditions under which they sold

their wheat. The farmer sold either to the local representatives of private merchant firms, whose headquarters were in Winnipeg (so that they could operate
on the Winnipeg Grain Exchange, or by telephone on
the other great wheat markets of the world), or to the
local elevator,[1] that is, warehouse, company, which
subsequently resold on the Winnipeg Exchange. The
farmers had a deep and growing conviction that they
got unnecessarily low prices, and that merchants and
speculators were making fortunes at their expense.
Before the war, however, the only concrete result of
this discontent was the formation of certain companies
by the farmers themselves, to which the term co-
operative was applied, though in fact they really operated
almost exactly like ordinary public joint stock companies. During the war, however, owing to the world
wheat shortage and the necessities of the Allied
countries, the whole system of private marketing was
displaced by a compulsory centralised system under
the Canada Wheat Board, the farmers being compelled
to deliver their wheat to the local elevators for disposal
by the Board: on delivery the farmers received a substantial first payment according to the grades which
each delivered, and as the Board sold, further payments were made. Thus the farmers eventually received
the full selling value of their wheat less the expenses of
the Board. This system met with widespread approval

---

[1] The lower illustration facing this page shows a large elevator at
the junction of rail and ship transport: the local elevator is simply a
smaller edition of this terminal elevator.

By courtesy of Oxford Institute for Research in Agricultural Engineering

A "combine-harvester"

By courtesy of the High Commissioner for Canada

A large terminal elevator

Cutting sugar cane in Cuba

amongst the farmers, though perhaps their views, as to its superiority over the old individual marketing to private firms, were somewhat coloured by the very high prices obtained during the war years. Consequently, there was a considerable agitation for its continuance after the war, but this naturally met with the bitter opposition of the Winnipeg merchants and their employees, and the Board was duly brought to an end.

The farmers, however, were determined not to return to the old system, and in 1923 a group in Alberta decided to adapt the war-time system into a voluntary co-operative marketing scheme. Farmers were invited to sign a contract pledging themselves to deliver their crops for the next five years to the co-operative society, which would pool the wheat obtained according to its graded quality, and sell it, as and when it deemed the conditions of the market were most propitious, withholding sales when either supplies were too abundant or the demand temporarily sub-normal, and selling freely in the reverse cases. It was argued that in many ways the co-operative society could improve on the prices obtainable by individual marketing, but in particular it would certainly prevent the seasonal slump in the weeks directly after the harvest, which was caused by the farmers' necessity to sell at once in order to get cash to pay for the expenses of harvesting and for the preparation of the ground for the new crop. Under the co-operative or pool system, the members would receive a substantial first payment on delivering their wheat at the local elevator, which would enable them to meet their current expenses, while the pool would not at once sell more than the market could readily absorb: the pool in fact would sell more or less regularly over the season, and so would obtain a better average price than individual farmers could obtain, because they were all virtually forced to sell a large proportion of their crop as soon as it was harvested, and therefore to sell at an unduly low price.

This scheme, for co-operative marketing by means of a pool, met with the approval of nearly half the farmers in Alberta, and was successfully put into operation in 1923. The other two prairie provinces followed suit in 1924, and the three provincial pools then formed a Central Selling Agency, composed of three representatives from each of them. In 1925 this agency marketed roughly half the total Canadian crop, and continued to market this amount, and more, for the next two years, the machinery working smoothly and satisfactorily, and the farmer members growing as pleased with the results as private merchants were disgruntled. Consequently, when the original five-year contracts expired during the early summer of 1928, they were almost all renewed, and additional new ones made, so that the pools now seemed thoroughly well-established institutions.

Then came the harvesting of the bumper crop of 1928. Possibly as an aid to securing the renewal of the contracts, but perhaps merely because they failed to realise fully the great size of the coming crop, the central selling agency of the pools carried over an appreciable amount of unsold wheat into the new season. This must be regarded as a serious mistake, for common-sense discretion dictated the advisability of reducing its carry-over to a minimum in view of the certainty that the coming crop would be above average, even though its exact size was still uncertain. It cannot however be maintained that if the Pool[1] had cleared its stocks, subsequent history would have been very different. As regards the 1928 crop itself the Pool shared with private speculators the view that the excess of supplies was a merely temporary condition and that, within a year or two, the bumper crop would be balanced by a short crop, while in any case the price had fallen low enough, and a rise was about to take place. Consequently the Pool restricted its sales to such amounts as the market would absorb at prices which, though considerably lower than the 1927–28 level, were never in danger of serious collapse. The result was that the Pool carried over extremely large stocks into the 1929–30 season, though once more it may be emphasised that private speculators were doing the same sort of thing. It may be argued that private speculators were really speculating not on the statistical situation of supply and demand but on the success of the Pool's operations; this however only means that they thought the Pool's view of the situation was

[1] Strictly speaking "the central selling agency of the pools". But since this had complete centralised control of all sales, it is legitimate and convenient to speak of "the Pool" in respect to selling policies, etc., and to use the plural only when the three member pools took individual action. This use is followed here.

fundamentally correct, since it is the statistical situation which must ultimately be the decisive factor in any long period speculation. In any case the combined result was that the world's carry-over on August 1st, 1929, was nearly double what it had been two years previously, and very considerably in excess of the normal amount, while the price was certainly far above what it would have been if the Pool had not held back its sales, and the private merchants and speculators had had to carry the whole available supplies. From this it has been argued, that much of the blame for subsequent disasters must rest on the Pool, on the grounds that if the price had fallen to the very low level which would have been reached in the latter part of 1928 but for the Pool's action, wheat producers would have appreciably contracted their acreage for the 1929 crop, and so there would not have been such excessive supplies when the world depression began. This line of argument cannot lightly be dismissed, but it may be urged in reply, that recent experience suggests that it takes more than one or even two seasons of extremely low prices to bring about any appreciable reduction of acreage in the big exporting countries, while there is no reason to suppose that the importing countries of Western Europe would have adopted any very different policy in respect of their domestic producers, if the collapse of wheat prices had occurred twelve to eighteen months earlier than it did. The real trouble was that the Pool was no wiser than the merchant speculator fraternity in diagnosing the underlying tendency to excess capacity, and no more able to foresee coming events.

In the autumn of 1929 the price of wheat was still around $1·50 per bushel, and the Pool can hardly be accused of rashness in fixing the initial payment to its members at $1. But by October–November the price was down to $1·25, and the three member pools felt compelled to ask for assurances that the banks would not force them to sell out in order that their loans to the pools might be recovered intact. The banks refused any such assurances, and so the pools applied to their respective provincial governments, who promptly guaranteed their accounts with the banks, for at the time no one dreamed that wheat could fall below $1. But during 1930 this happened, and in the end the receipts from selling the 1929 crop fell short of the total advances paid to the members by about 23 million dollars. The provincial governments met this loss in the main by issuing state bonds to the banks, on the security of the mortgages on the elevators owned by the pools, who agreed to pay them off over a period of years out of the earnings of the elevators.

We now come to the 1930–31 crop. The Pool made an initial advance in the early autumn of 1930 of 60 cents per bushel, the price then fluctuating round about 1 dollar: a little later this was reduced to 55 cents. But the price went on falling, and it was clear that if the Pool attempted to sell its total holdings, the price would completely collapse, for private merchant-speculators were now thoroughly frightened. Such a complete collapse virtually meant the collapse of the whole economic organisation of the country. So, with the backing of the three provincial governments, the pools appealed to the Dominion Government. But the Dominion Government would only assist on condition that they would accept a general manager, nominated by itself and approved by the banks, who was to have an unfettered dictatorship in selling both the accumulated stocks and the 1930 crop. Since the only alternative was certain bankruptcy, the pools had to accept, and in November 1930 Mr J. I. McFarland was appointed as dictator.

Mr McFarland was a wheat merchant, and naturally therefore he preferred to work through "the private trade". Accordingly, the Pool's methods of direct export through its own offices overseas were brought to an end, though the change-over gave rise to considerable difficulties and complaints from millers in the United Kingdom and Germany. Otherwise, the general pool system was carried on. Then in the spring of 1931, the Dominion Government appointed a Royal Commission under the chairmanship of Sir Josiah Stamp to report on the whole system of speculative markets and dealing in wheat. The Commission pronounced very definitely in favour of the indispensability and positive merits of the merchant-speculator regime, but there is no need for us to attempt to pass judgment on this report because, whether it was sound or unsound, there is no doubt that it failed to carry any conviction among the farmers, and created a political storm at Ottawa.

Consequently, another investigation of the whole wheat-marketing problem was held, this time by the Agricultural Committee of the Canadian legislature. The private grain merchants maintained that they could market the crop satisfactorily. The representatives of the pools argued that nothing but the pool system, adequately financed, could prevent a serious fall in price in the autumn, when the farmers were forced to sell their crop at once in order to obtain cash, and advocated the creation of a national wheat board similar to that which had been in operation during the war. The private grain trade replied that if there were such a seasonal price-fall, the Government could relieve the pressure of supplies by directing Mr McFarland to enter the market as a buyer. Eventually the Government decided against the scheme for a national wheat board. Thereupon the pools, realising that they could not obtain adequate finance from the banks to make initial payments to their members on a scale sufficient to enable them to carry on, cancelled the contracts of their members, leaving them free to sell the 1931 crop and all subsequent crops to anyone they wished.

Thus ended the great experiment of the Canadian Wheat Pools. The pools remain in being, but only as the owners and operators of elevators, and as such they carry on business just in the same way as do the private elevator companies, though of course on a vastly larger scale; as owners of elevators the pools have fared relatively well. A certain number of small new pools have been organised, but they must now operate exactly as do private merchants, since otherwise they cannot obtain finance from the banks. The Central Selling Agency has really become a government department for the liquidation of the stocks held when the pooling system was brought to an end, and as the organisation through which the Canadian Government has been attempting to control the Winnipeg market during the last four years. It is not proposed to examine its operations in detail, because the necessary data are not yet fully available. But it may be said that Mr McFarland has bought wheat, not only when this seemed necessary to prevent a further collapse in the price, which has more than once threatened, but also in an endeavour to force up the price to a definitely higher level. In this he has been largely successful, for during the last two years the price of Canadian wheat has been very substantially higher than the general price-level of Argentine or Australian wheat. But this has only been done at a considerable cost to the Canadian Government, and possibly to the detriment of the future of the wheat industry of Canada. On August 1st, 1935, the Canadian Government was carrying 200 million bushels out of a total world carry-over of a little more than 800 million bushels; Canadian stocks were actually higher on August 1st, 1935, than a year before, despite the curtailment of world supplies by the 1934 drought: moreover, Canada was practically the only country with stocks over and above the normal carry-over from one season to another. In short, the surplus wheat stocks of the world were concentrated in Canada, while the world only demands Canadian wheat when no other alternative supplies are available, and this is not a healthy position for any exporter.

Opinion in Canada was indeed becoming alarmed at the whole problem. In July a new Wheat Act had been passed, establishing a National Grain Board, which was, *inter alia*, to take over the Government's stocks of wheat, and sell them as quickly as possible. Thus a change of policy seemed imminent, but the outlook was that the exportable surplus of the 1935–36 crop would be considerably in excess of requirements, and therefore the liquidation of the stocks, at anything near the existing price-level, seemed only a remote possibility.

But during August and September the whole outlook was completely changed. The disease known as "Black Rust" is attacking the crop on an unprecedented scale. As a result, the world price has risen by 20 per cent. since July, and is still rising now in mid-September. It is now estimated that the 1935 crop will not be much larger than that of 1934, i.e. about 275 million bushels as compared with a normal of about 400 million. It should therefore be possible for the new Grain Board to liquidate most of Canada's surplus stocks during the present season, and after all the Canadian Government may win its colossal gamble.

Postscript, December 14th, 1935. The last three months has confirmed the views expressed immediately above, and it is now virtually certain that the world will require to draw largely on Canada's stocks before the present season finishes.

Chapter IV

CONTROL SCHEMES IN SUGAR

"EAST is East and West is West" even in the world trade in sugar, for normally the sugar grown in each hemisphere is consumed in that hemisphere, and there is not much trade between them. Now in each hemisphere, there are a number of countries which produce the whole, or a large part, of their sugar requirements, and also there is one country which normally supplies the major part of the balance required by these countries, and also the requirements of those countries which produce very little or no sugar; these big exporters are Java in the East, and Cuba in the West. In the Western hemisphere, ten years ago, when all the present troubles may be said to have started, the continental countries of Europe as a group produced nearly all the sugar they required. Most of them grew some sugar, and Czechoslovakia and Poland grew more than they wanted themselves, and were usually able to supply the deficiencies of their neighbours. On the other hand, Great Britain imported practically all its sugar—well over one-third came from Cuba, and the balance mainly from our colonies and dominions. The other great importing country was the United States, for even including the Hawaiian Islands and the Philippines, which are inside the American tariff wall, the United States produced little more than one-half of its requirements: it imported the other half from Cuba which enjoyed a preference in the American tariff schedule. Putting it very broadly, the position ten years ago was that the United States and the United Kingdom were the big importers, and Cuba the big exporter. Similarly, in the Eastern hemisphere Java was the big exporter, making up the requirements of India, Japan and China over and above their home production. Of course very many other countries produced sugar, in nearly all cases behind high tariffs, but they had little or no surplus to export, and were of little account in the world trade in sugar. For further details about the channels along which sugar is distributed, reference should be made to the map on pp. 88–89.

The next thing to be considered is the distinction between sugar produced from beet and sugar produced from sugar cane. Until the disturbances of the last five years, rather less than one-half of the world's sugar was produced from beet, and, therefore, rather more than one-half from sugar cane. It is, of course, beet-sugar which is produced in Europe, and about one-third of the production within the United States tariff wall is also beet-sugar. Practically speaking all the other countries produce cane-sugar. There is probably no need to say very much here about the cultivation of beet-sugar; the seed has to be sown each spring, and the main work is singling out the plants and weeding through the early stages of growth: then, of course, in the autumn the roots are lifted. It

is much like growing beet as a vegetable, except that
the roots are white instead of red. Few people in the
British Isles, however, have seen sugar cane, because
it can only be cultivated in or near the tropics. Small
lengths of cane are put in the ground in rows, and
these shoot up in due course, and grow until they
become a thick mass of canes essentially like a corn-
field, only the stalks or canes are from 1 to $1\frac{1}{2}$ inches
thick and 6 to 10 feet high, with a bunch of big
green leaves at the top instead of an ear. A certain
amount of weeding is required in the early stages of
growth, but once the cane has fairly started to grow,
it more or less takes care of itself. The harvesting[1] of
the crop, however, involves a great deal of labour. No
machine has yet been devised to cut the canes, which
has to be done by hand, and the tops have also to be
sliced off, as these contain very little sugar. Then the
bare canes are collected together and transported to
the factory. One qualification must, however, be made
concerning the setting of the small pieces of cane in
the ground to sprout. That is done each season in
certain countries, notably in Java, but in Cuba and the
West Indian Islands there is no need to do this; the
old roots are left in the ground after the cane has been
cut, and these roots throw up new shoots when the
rains come. This is what is known as "ratooning", and,
of course, where it can be practised, there is an
enormous saving in the costs of production. In Cuba,
on new land, it is usually unnecessary to replant for

[1] See illustration facing page 65.

ten or more years, though on land which has been used for a long time, replanting must take place every three or four years.

This difference is indeed only one factor in the radically different character of the sugar industries of the two great exporting countries. In Cuba, for example, the average yield of sugar is about 1½ tons per acre: in Java, on the other hand, it is as much as 5 tons per acre. And yet Cuba and Java can grow sugar at much the same cost. Put into technical terms, we say that the cultivation in Cuba is extensive, and in Java intensive. The point is that in Cuba there is plenty of land, but until recently not too much labour was available, and what there was, being mainly white, was relatively expensive. On the other hand, in Java land is scarce relative to the huge native population, and labour is plentiful and cheap. Consequently the Cuban industry achieves low costs by relying mainly on nature, whereas Java achieves low costs by the application of much capital and labour in extremely scientific and intensive cultivation. Other cane-growing countries, in this respect, may be said to come somewhere between these two extremes, with the exception of Hawaii where the cultivation is even more intensive than in Java, though for rather different reasons.

Turning to the factory part of the industry, the growing of cane and the manufacture of sugar are usually under separate control. Most cane-sugar mills are owned by joint stock companies, and they buy their cane from a very large number of small cane farmers, just as in the same way a beet-sugar factory buys its roots from farmers over a wide radius round it. The principal exceptions are in Java and Hawaii, where the companies grow their own cane, because of the absence of a class of farmers able to maintain the highly scientific standard of cultivation required. The process of manufacture is essentially the same for cane and beet-roots: both are ground and sliced up so as to extract the juice, which is then boiled in order to extract the sugar, the resulting sugar liquid being purified up to a point, and finally crystallised. Refining simply carries this process of purification further. Refineries, however, are usually situated in the countries of consumption, in order to suit the varying tastes and fashions of different nations in the matter of their sugar.

With these preliminaries, we can now start on the story of the sugar industry in recent years. Though it now seems a long time ago, it is absolutely necessary to go back to the Great War years, because fighting took place over a large part of the best beet areas of the European continent, and the final result of the war years was to reduce the European beet-sugar crop from 8 million tons to $2\frac{1}{2}$ million tons. Many readers will remember that during the war there was a chronic shortage of sugar in all countries, and rationing schemes had to be introduced. Now Cuba was almost the only country where the expansion of sugar production could take place rapidly to meet this deficiency, and during the last two years of the war, there was an enormous amount of new planting of hitherto uncultivated land in the middle and eastern end of the island; so much so, that whereas Cuba's pre-war crop was about 2½ million tons, in 1918 Cuba produced 4 million tons. During 1919 and the beginning of 1920, the whole world was trying to replenish its sugar stocks, the available supplies were quite insufficient, and there was a terrific boom in the price. The peak was reached in May 1920, when the price of raw sugar was about 10d. per pound —incidentally, it should be noted, and remembered, that all the prices of sugar which are quoted in this chapter are approximate only, and in all cases refer to *raw* and not refined sugar, still less to refined sugar as it is retailed by the grocer. Of course, a price of 10d. per pound meant untold wealth to Cuba, where this boom was popularly called "The Dance of the Millions". But then came the post-war depression, and there was an almost equally terrific slump in the price of sugar, so that by December 1920, eight months later, it was down to 2d. and a year later, in December 1921, to 1d. per pound. This post-war depression, however, was comparatively short, and at the beginning of 1923 the price was back again at 2d.; and that was quite reasonably profitable for nearly all the Cuban mills, and extremely profitable for the large new mills in the east of the island, whose costs were only about one-half as great as those of the older mills in the west. These older mills were on too small a scale, while the lands from which they obtained their cane were becoming exhausted.

Now, from 1919 to 1928, the rate of the recovery of

the European beet-sugar industry had been slow, but, under the stimulus of high tariffs, in the next two years it became very rapid. The Cuban producers did not foresee this, and at the same time as this rapid recovery was taking place in Europe, they were also increasing their acreage. Several other producing countries made the same mistake, but since they were mostly within the United States tariff wall, the mistake did not cost them so dearly as it was to cost Cuba. The combined result was that, in the season 1924–25, the world's production of sugar jumped up tremendously, and though consumption was rapidly increasing, it could not keep pace with this sudden increase in production, and the price of raw sugar fell back to about $1\frac{1}{4}d.$ per pound. A price of $1\frac{1}{4}d.$ per pound was well below the costs of most of the Cuban producers at that time. Moreover, it seemed certain that in the next year production would be still greater, and the price still lower. The only hope seemed to be for Cuba to restrict the size of the coming crop, and eventually this was done by government decree to the extent of 10 per cent. That was the beginning of a policy of restriction which was eventually to become more or less world-wide.

It is impossible here to enter upon a detailed study of the Cuban restriction schemes during the next few years, though it is an interesting story. Looking back now, we can see that the policy of restriction was bound to fail, for it was, so to speak, a case of Cuba against the world, and a world in which almost every country was determined to be self-sufficient in the matter of its sugar supplies, no matter what the cost. As Cuba diminished her crops by more and more severe restriction, her chief customers increased their home production under the stimulus of tariffs and bounties, and her competitors in the export trade benefited by the fact that the price was higher than it would have been if the Cuban crop had not been restricted. At the end of 1928, disgust at the failure of restriction to raise prices, or even to stop their falling, resulted in the abandonment of all restrictions on the Cuban crop of 1929. And in that year good weather almost all over the world resulted in record crops everywhere, and the price of raw sugar fell below 1d. per pound. To crown everything came the Wall Street crash in the autumn, and for some time the United States practically stopped buying sugar. The result was the accumulation of enormous stocks in Cuba, and by mid-1930 the price of raw sugar was only just above ½d. a lb.

Opinion in Cuba had rapidly veered round again in favour of restriction during 1929, but it was now obvious that restriction by Cuba alone was useless. Ever since she began restriction, Cuba had been trying to get the other big exporting countries to follow her example. But Java had always refused to agree because, there, a new variety of cane had recently been introduced which gave a yield of sugar some 30 per cent. greater than the varieties which had hitherto been planted; and this, of course, meant such a reduction of costs that Java thought she could sell at a profit even the much bigger crops yielded by the new cane. And while

Java stood out, the European countries would not join Cuba in establishing a restriction scheme for fear lest Java should dump very cheap sugar into Europe. But by 1930 Java was finding it impossible to sell her crop, and was herself afraid lest Cuba should dump in her Eastern markets. The very low price, and the diminishing consumption everywhere, made some combined action seem desirable to all, and so, after many conferences, in May 1931, an international agreement was signed by the chief exporting countries, providing for the restriction of exports, and the gradual disposal of surplus stocks, over a period of five years. The countries concerned were Germany, Czechoslovakia, Poland, Hungary, Belgium, Cuba, Java and Peru, and the agreement is commonly referred to as the Chadbourne Scheme, after the American who was the prime mover in the whole matter. Under the terms of the scheme the production in each country was limited to its current home requirements whatever they might be, plus an agreed export quota.

The Chadbourne Scheme was hailed as the beginning of a new era for the world's sugar industry, but such optimism was short-lived. The price continued to decline. Taking the average price of raw sugar imported into Great Britain, which is probably the best single measurement of sugar prices in recent years, we find that the average for the season 1930–31 (ending August 31st) was 6s. 4d. per cwt., for 1931–32 5s. 10d., for 1932–33 5s. 3d., for 1933–34 4s. 9d., and for last season about 4s. 6d. There were of course considerable fluctuations: a low level was reached in April 1932, but this was followed by a sharp recovery, owing to the anticipated effects of such low prices combined with a reduction which was then made in Cuba's quota under the Chadbourne Scheme. But from August 1932 until August 1934, a slowly declining trend was resumed, becoming more rapid during the autumn of 1934, until in November a record low level was reached at 3s. 10d. per cwt. But this was partly due to seasonal influences, and there was again a fairly sharp recovery, only to be followed once more by another slow decline during the summer of 1935. Thus the Chadbourne Scheme miserably failed to secure its objective of raising the price. The other main objective, to effect a reduction of the enormous stocks, was however in part achieved, for on August 31st, 1935, stocks were about 1½ million tons less than in 1931, when they totalled no less than 7½ million tons. Even so, the 1935 stocks were more than twice as great as the normal ratio to current consumption. Nearly half these stocks are in Cuba and Java, and these are really the surplus stocks, for at the end of the season these producing countries would normally carry-over merely nominal amounts. Thus the Chadbourne Scheme as a whole met with little success, and when the causes of its failure are examined, it is hardly surprising that it was not renewed on the completion of the period of five years (Sept. 1st, 1935) for which it was originally concluded.

The principal cause of failure of the Chadbourne Scheme was the increase of production by countries outside the agreement, that is in the main by the Chadbourne countries' customers. This went far to neutralise the tremendous restriction of exports which the Chadbourne countries imposed upon themselves, and faithfully observed. Thus the output of the Chadbourne countries was reduced by nearly 7 million tons per annum, while the output of the rest of the world was increased by about 4½ million tons. Of this increased production, about 1½ million tons came from the United States and its island possessions, and the remainder from the British Empire. Such an enormous increase was not fully anticipated by the Chadbourne countries, who therefore consistently under-estimated the degree of restriction required, though it is doubtful whether they could have restricted much more severely than they actually did, even if they had realised the need. For the Cuban crop was in fact reduced to a little over 2 million tons as compared with over 5 million in 1929, and in 1934 Java produced only 700,000 tons as compared with over 3 million, while the European members produced little more than half their 1929 output. The result of the increased production by the United States and the British Empire was therefore to reduce the requirements of importing countries below even the apparently conservative estimates on which the Chadbourne Scheme was based, and this decline in importers' requirements— or the increase in their domestic production, for the two come to the same thing—so neutralised the restriction of output under the scheme, that, though some reduction of stocks did result, large surplus stocks still remained, and consequently the price failed to rise; instead, it declined in sympathy with the continual shrinkage in import requirements.

All this increase of production in the United States and the British Empire took place of course behind tariff walls or with the help of bounties, and the failure of the Chadbourne Scheme was thus due not to inherent defects in the scheme itself or in its administration, but simply to the growing strength of economic nationalism in respect of sugar. Indeed, economic nationalism has been the fundamental cause of all the troubles of sugar and sugar exporters not merely since 1931, but since 1925. The essence of the whole sugar problem has, all along, been the determination of almost every country in the world to produce its own sugar, more or less irrespective of the cost. The European and American beet-sugar industries have always, right from their start, owed their continued existence to protective tariffs or subsidies; and these have been given for two main reasons: first, the desirability of home-grown supplies of sugar in the event of war, or of a serious world shortage of sugar; and, secondly, the technical benefits of beet sugar as a rotation crop in farming, and the fact that it necessitates a great deal of labour, for most countries have wanted to stop the decline in their rural population. Now the Great War of 1914–18, and the sugar shortage of 1919–20, emphasised the first reason, and the almost world-wide difficulties in agriculture from, say, 1923 onwards emphasised the employment aspect. If agriculturalists were to be helped, what better way could there be than to subsidise a crop which demands a relatively large expenditure on wages, and at the same time ensures to the consumer at least part of his usual supplies in time of war or shortage? This mixture of political and social reasons has been responsible for the development of beet-sugar production in many countries where none had been produced before, and of cane-sugar production in countries where beet sugar could not be grown. As the home industries grew, so each country imported less and less, and so naturally the world price of sugar fell. As the price fell, the degree of subsidy or protection had to be increased in order to preserve the home industries, which had been developed at such a cost to the tax-payer or the consumer, while in some cases further expansion has been stimulated, in order to increase agricultural employment and assist the general farmer. The position in 1935 has become almost incredible. The price of raw sugar at British ports is round about 4s. 6d. per cwt.: home-grown sugar in Great Britain receives a total assistance by the combined effect of the tariff and the subsidy of just under 12s. per cwt.: so that it costs British consumers nearly *three* times as much to *grow* their own sugar as they might buy it for. Colonial and Dominion sugars receive preferential tariff rates which are rather complicated, but one may say very broadly that on the average they receive a preference of nearly 100 per cent., i.e. Colonial and Dominion sugar costs Great Britain twice as much as if bought in the world market. In the United States,

the price of raw sugar in the summer of 1935 was about
1·80 cents per lb.: the full tariff duty was 1·87 cents,
but Cuban sugar pays only half the full rate, and so the
practical and effective protection to United States
home producers was only about 50 per cent.; but until
May 1934 it was enormously more. The extreme case,
I think, has been South Africa, which was at one time
exporting nearly 40 per cent. of its total production at
a price of about 8s. a cwt., and charging its home
consumers 30s. a cwt. for the remainder in order to
cover the total costs. Australia has been nearly, if not
quite, as extreme. But it should be made clear that in
general, countries under the British or American flags
are not much, if any, more extreme than many other
countries. The result of this determination to be self-
sufficient in sugar supplies, combined with the effect on
consumption of artificially high prices in a time of
world depression, is that little more than one-quarter
as much sugar is now required from Cuba and Java.
Their industries are virtually ruined, while consumers
the world over are paying enormously more for their
sugar than they need. Of course, neither Cuba nor
Java can produce profitably at the present price, but
they are easily the world's cheapest producers, and in
a sense it is because of their low costs that they have
been ruined. And it must be realised that Cuba at
least could probably produce double its present record
production. There is still plenty of new fertile land, and
Cuba could certainly supply the United States, Great
Britain and a large slice of Europe at a cost far below

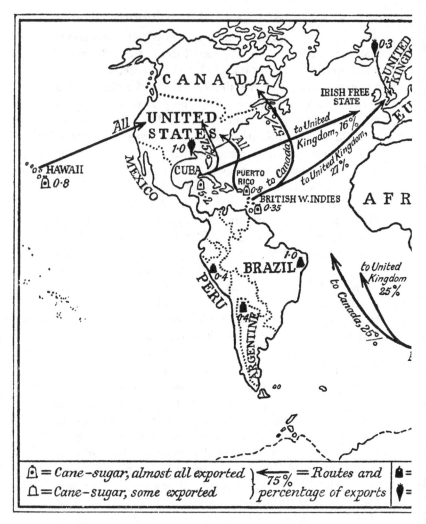

0.3

CANADA

UNITED
STATES

IRISH FREE
STATE

All

1.0

75%

All

to United
Kingdom, 16%

HAWAII
0.8

CUBA

MEXICO

PUERTO
RICO
0.8

to United Kingdom,
27%

to Canada

0.8

BRITISH W.INDIES
0.35

AFR

5.2

1.0

BRAZIL

PERU

0.4

to United
Kingdom
25%

to Canada, 25%

ARGENTINE

0.4

0.0

THE WORLD'S SU

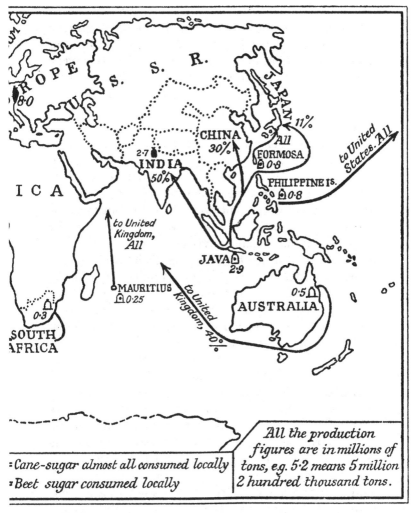

to United States. All

to United Kingdom, All

to United Kingdom, 40%

All the production figures are in millions of tons, e.g. 5·2 means 5 million 2 hundred thousand tons.

= Cane-sugar almost all consumed locally
= Beet sugar consumed locally

GAR CROPS, 1929

the cost of home production in these countries. Similarly, Java could supply British India, Malaya, and so on. Cuba, Java, and some of the other very cheap cane-sugar producing countries, could together supply the whole world at prices far below the cost of production of most of the sugar being made to-day.

That is the general situation and the fundamental problem with which exporters have been attempting to deal by establishing artificial control schemes. Assuming that this economic nationalism was no temporary phenomenon, but was likely to continue and probably to increase at any rate for a period as far ahead as anyone could envisage, it is clear that restriction could never be a cure for their troubles. The object of restriction is to preserve productive capacity intact, whereas in Cuba and Java, and other exporting countries, equilibrium could never be regained except by a drastic amputation of capacity. Precisely in so far as restriction schemes were successful, they would merely draw out the agony, or at best postpone the inevitable. But it may be argued that in Cuba and Java the excess of capacity by 1931 was so great that sudden amputation by a drastic fall of price, such as would probably have occurred in the absence of the Chadbourne Scheme, would have utterly smashed the whole economic life of these countries, whereas under the Chadbourne Scheme the process has been gradual, and therefore less catastrophic. This line of argument may well be true up to a point; the Chadbourne

Scheme may then be judged, not as a means to victory, but as a means of ensuring an orderly retreat, and as such it should probably receive qualified approval. But it should nevertheless be realised that this approval rests upon the failure of the scheme as originally conceived. If the price had been raised and stocks reduced to normal, there would not have been the steady pressure under which producing units have been squeezed to death during the last five years because they could not carry on at the low price coupled with such severe restriction: on the contrary, existing capacity would have been preserved, and the evil day would merely have been postponed. It is precisely because the Chadbourne Scheme failed to reach its objectives, that it can probably be justified as an improvement on *laissez-faire* under the conditions of the last few years. It was not renewed because it was no longer effective even as a means of covering its members' retreat, and because the members felt that nothing was to be gained by further collective action, and that the time had come for them to fight out amongst themselves which of them should supply what remained of the world market. In such a fight, Cuba hopes that the limitation of domestic production by the United States, coupled with the increased preference which was given to Cuban sugar in 1934, will give her some advantage. What will now happen with unrestricted production remains to be seen, but there are unfortunately few signs that the world will shortly return to a more common-sense organisation of its sugar supplies, and it therefore looks as if exporters must adjust themselves somehow to a more or less permanent continuation of the existing *status quo*.

Postscript, December 14th, 1935. There has been no development of outstanding importance since September, though the price of sugar has increased from about 4*s*. 6*d*. to a 5*s*. level. Attention may also be drawn to the proposed reorganisation of the U.K. beet-sugar industry and the revision of the subsidy.

Chapter V

COTTON is grown in more than one hundred different countries, spread all over the world's tropical and sub-tropical regions. But there are only five of these countries which produce more than one million bales a year—the United States, India, China, Egypt and Russia. Together these five countries produce nearly 90 per cent. of the world's supplies of cotton. Of these big producers, the United States towers over the others, producing on the average about 55 per cent. of the total world crop, or in the five years ending 1929 about 16 million bales a year. India is the next biggest producer with an average crop of about 5·5 million bales, China next with nearly 2 million, and then comes Egypt with about 1·5 million bales, and Russia with about 1 million in 1928 and 1929, and considerably more in the last few years. As nearly 60 per cent. of the United States, or as it is commonly called the American, crop is exported, American cotton also dominates the international trade in cotton. Moreover from the point of view of artificial control schemes, it is of course the recent control of the American cotton crop which is of such outstanding importance and interest, though Egypt has also made some interesting experiments. Hence in this chapter attention will be concentrated almost exclusively on the American cotton industry, and account will be taken of the cotton industries of other countries only in so far as is necessary and desirable for a proper understanding of the American story.

The cotton plant has to be sown each year, and its successful cultivation requires a great deal of rain during the growing season, but an absolute drought during the picking season as rain would then discolour and damage the cotton fibre. The United States "cotton belt" stretches from the States of South Carolina and Georgia on the Atlantic right across the great valley of the Mississippi and through the State of Texas: roughly 1000 miles from east to west and 400–500 miles from north to south. Naturally the climatic conditions, and therefore the time of sowing, varies, but if the seed is sown, say, in March, by May the plants begin to flower, and as the flowers die, a round seed-pod gradually develops until it is about 1 inch in diameter. About August this seed-pod, or as it is termed "boll", begins to open, and inside the boll is seen a mass of seeds each attached to a light fibre, varying from a little under to a little over 1 inch in length. Nature of course attached this fibre to the seed so that it would float on the wind, and thus be scattered as widely as possible. When the boll is sufficiently wide open, its bulging contents are picked,[1] but for two or three months fresh bolls are maturing in succession, and so the plants have to be picked over more or less continuously, and altogether the picking season lasts three

[1] See illustrations facing page 157.

or four months. Now of course the seed comes away with the fibres, and so when the grower has collected a load, he takes it to the local ginnery, where the seed is torn off the fibres by machinery, and the fibres are then compressed and packed into bales of cotton "lint" destined to be spun and woven into cotton manufactures. The ginning is sometimes done for a definite price, but quite commonly the ginnery keeps the seed as its remuneration. The seed still has little bits of fibre attached, and further processes get this off, and the little bits, known as "linters", are then similarly baled: linters are too short to be spun, but are used for wadding, for the manufacture of blotting paper, for making artificial silk and other purposes. From the clean seed, oils, meal, cattle cake and so on are manufactured.

Before we consider the marketing of the bales of cotton proper, that is lint cotton, we must first get some idea of the sort of people who grow it. In the main American cotton is, and always has been, grown by quite small farmers, of whom a very large proportion are negroes: there are very few large-scale plantations running into hundreds or even thousands of acres, such as one finds in coffee or rubber and sometimes in sugar. The reason for this small-scale farming lies in the very uneven amount of labour which the cotton crop requires at different seasons. The plants need a good deal of attention and labour during the early growing season, then for a couple of months or so comparatively little, and finally a great deal of labour is required for the actual picking, because this has to be done entirely by hand: no satisfactory machine has yet been invented, despite innumerable experiments. Thus the maximum requirement of labour is several times as great as the minimum, and if cotton were grown on large plantations, there would either be a chronic shortage of workers during the two busy times, and especially during the picking season, or there would be a chronic surplus of workers during most of the year. But a small farmer, working directly for himself, will do far more than a normal day's work for a short period, and in addition he can call on his wife and children to help at the busiest time, since the art of cotton picking is easily learned. Thus small-scale family farming solves the labour problem involved in cotton production in a way which is far cheaper, and far more effective, than would be possible under large-scale planting. And so we find that the American cotton crop is grown by well over one million individual farmers, vast numbers of whom do not produce more than five or ten bales a year, even though cotton is their principal crop.

This small-scale family farming involves a huge and most difficult financial problem, for such farmers, the world over, are universally short of capital. In the United States the owners of the land sometimes find the working capital for their negro tenants in the shape of seeds, manures, animals and implements, and receive interest at the end of the season in the form of a share of the cotton produced. But this sort of thing is exceptional; the vast bulk of the cotton farmers must borrow, and since they can rarely provide security of a type which banks consider suitable, they are forced to borrow from local storekeepers, merchants, and small moneylenders, on the security of their growing crop. Thus very commonly the local storekeeper is also really a cotton merchant, and he provides the farmers with their agricultural requirements, and with the requirements of themselves and their families during the growing season, on condition that he gets the first refusal to purchase their crop. Such storekeepers naturally have to charge a high rate of interest, for the investment of their capital in this way is a highly risky business depending in large part on the weather. But the real trouble is that the storekeeper often comes to hold a whip hand over the entire fortunes of the farmer and his family, and can then bleed him unmercifully in a variety of ways. Conditions have been greatly altered since the Government began its control schemes in 1929, but even now a great proportion of the growers are mortgaged up to the hilt with local shopkeepers and merchants.

This brings us back to the marketing of his cotton by the farmer. As has been said, the local storekeepers sometimes buy the farmer's cotton, or it may be bought by local merchants whose business is as much money-lending as merchanting. Again, there may be small independent buyers who make a living by buying cotton in the local market, and reselling it by telephone the same day to larger merchants at larger up-country centres. None of these local or up-country buyers is in fact likely to hold his purchases for more than a few days, and will quickly resell to larger merchants or exporters, whose headquarters will be at one of the cotton seaports. Such firms, in addition to buying from the local merchants and dealers, may themselves send their own representatives to the local markets. Thus the economic function of all the local buyers is to collect the crop from the innumerable growers all over the belt, and concentrate it into the hands of a relatively small number of large merchants.

Now it is the subsequent selling of the crop by these large merchants in the big markets like New Orleans, New York and Liverpool, which may be said to determine the general price-level of cotton: prices in the little local markets follow, rather than lead, this world price-level. But the farmer is of course concerned directly with the price which he gets in his local market, and the settlement of the individual bargains between farmer and local buyer was, at least until recently, a very haphazard affair. For when the farmer brings a load of cotton away from the ginnery and takes it to the local market town, he has only the roughest idea as to its quality, and probably only a very general and somewhat out-of-date knowledge of the present level of prices on the big world markets. Equally the local buyer can form only the roughest idea from the sample which he draws from one of the bales as to the quality of the whole load, though he probably has a very much better knowledge of the movement of prices. He has indeed a fairly clear notion of the average price he is willing to pay for good, medium and low-grade cotton considered together, and since he cannot be sure of the exact quality of the particular loads he buys during the day, he will try to buy as near this average price as possible, hoping that by getting the good quality loads cheap, he will balance out the unduly high price which he has unwittingly paid for loads which eventually prove to be low quality. This "hog-round" price system therefore fails to give the skilful grower a proper reward for his good quality cotton, and on the other hand, unduly rewards the grower of low-grade cotton. But, apart from this, it is doubtful whether the growers as a body get the true average value of their cotton: as has been said, the buyers know much more about prices in the big markets, and they usually know more about the prices which other buyers in the market are offering than the seller can easily ascertain, while the formation of buyers' "rings" to prevent undue competition amongst themselves is often only too easy in the smaller markets. All in all, the conditions of primary marketing in cotton were, until recently, not only chaotic, but almost certainly unfair to the growers. As will be explained later, the improvement of these conditions was one of the main objects of the co-operative associations which were formed after the war, and which were later so greatly developed under the Government's control schemes.

We must now consider briefly the factors influencing the world price of cotton. On the supply side, the crop

will of course depend in the first instance on the acreage
sown each year, and this is likely to be much influenced
by the price-level ruling at the time, that is, the price
of the previous crop. Thus a high price in the spring
of one year tends to bring about the sowing of a high
acreage, and if the weather is normal, a large crop
follows, and this tends therefore to fetch a low price,
and so the next year's acreage is likely to be smaller,
and to send the price higher, and so on. There is
therefore a tendency towards an oscillation of high and
low prices, and large and small crops, all other factors
remaining the same. But though this tendency is well
worth noting, other factors do not in practice often
remain the same, and this is especially true of the
weather. The weather in the American cotton belt
varies a great deal from year to year, and consequently
a high acreage does not necessarily mean a large crop,
nor a low acreage a small crop. And as well as the
weather, there is the effect of damage by the seventy
different kinds of insects which prey upon the cotton
plant. Of these the boll-weevil is by far the worst, and
in certain seasons since the war has reduced the crop
by 20 and even 30 per cent. Indeed, from 1921 to
1929, the boll-weevil was a decisive factor in determining the size of the crop, for in some years it
flourished and did enormous damage, as in 1921–23, and
then for the next three seasons it almost disappeared,
returning again however in 1927 for another three years.
Thus the American crop varies greatly in size from year
to year, partly on account of variations in the acreage

sown, and partly as the result of the weather and of insect damage: for example, in 1921 it was under 8 million bales, but as much as 18 million bales in 1926, and then it dropped to 13 million in 1927.

The demand for American cotton depends of course in the first place on the general consumption of the types of cotton goods manufactured from American cotton, and this is undoubtedly greatly influenced by the current price-level of those goods. A large proportion of the consumers of cotton cloth are poor people in India, China and Africa, and if cotton cloth is cheap, they will buy more than in proportion to the fall in price. Again, cotton is in competition with other textile materials, such as wool, and in recent years particularly with artificial silk. The changes in the consumption of cotton since the war provide unmistakable evidence of the sensitiveness of the demand to changing prices. But we must not forget that different countries produce different kinds of raw cotton, and that within limits, though only within limits, these different kinds are interchangeable from the manufacturers' point of view. Thus if the price of American cotton, owing to a short crop, rises relatively to the price of Indian cotton, spinners of low-grade yarns will, so far as they can, use Indian cotton instead of American cotton, even though the latter suits them best, and similarly spinners of higher-grade yarns will use the normally more expensive Egyptian cotton. They can do this within limits, but only within limits, though the limits nowadays are much wider than they used to be, say, twenty or thirty years ago. It follows therefore that a small American crop will not fetch as high a price as it would do if cotton from other countries could not be substituted for American cotton at all. On the other hand, because the substitution can only take place within limits, it also follows that if the American crop is, say, 20 per cent. below normal, and the other crops of the world are so unusually good as to make up the difference, the price of American cotton will still go above normal; while because some substitution can take place, the abnormally great supply of other cottons will not fetch so low a price as it would if no substitution at all were possible. Thus variations in the American crop cannot under any circumstances be wholly balanced by opposite variations in the other cotton crops of the world, but they may be balanced in part, and the same applies to variations in those other crops *vis-à-vis* the American crop. Actually most of the other crops of the world vary less than the American crop, and thus the size of the American crop, and consequently its price, is normally a decisive factor in determining the general price-level of all cottons.

The course of American cotton prices from 1919 to 1929 may be summarised as follows. During the post-war boom, supplies were short and the demand so tremendous in its intensity that the price during the 1919–20 season averaged over 25*d*. per lb. The boom ended in the early autumn of 1920 just as much larger supplies were becoming available, and for the 1920–21 season the price averaged under 12*d*. But there was a rapid recovery because for the next three years boll-weevil damage was serious, and the supply of American cotton hardly kept pace with the demand until after the big crop of 1925, so that the price was very sensitive and fluctuated between 11*d*. and 17*d*. Following another big crop in 1926, the price went down to 8*d*., but with a short crop in 1927 it rose again, and with an average crop in 1928 remained at a level between 10*d*. and 11*d*. until the autumn of 1929. It cannot be said that, before the world depression began, the acreage under cotton was excessive, if one assumes an average amount of damage by the boll-weevil: but since this damage varied so greatly, the industry was perpetually see-sawing between a shortage and an excess of supplies, and any sort of equilibrium was as short-lived as it was precariously balanced.

Armed with this summary of general information, let us now tackle the very complex story of the successive experiments in the artificial control of the supplies of American cotton which the United States Government has been undertaking in recent years. I feel I must warn the reader that the rest of this chapter is not particularly easy reading, since it seems desirable to relate the story in some detail, partly because this is necessary for a proper explanation of how and why the United States Government was led on step by step into ever more ambitious aims, ever more extensive control, and ever greater financial commitments, and partly because the importance of cotton as one of the

greatest of the world's staple raw materials, and therefore the importance of experiments in its control,
justifies thorough and careful study. When the reader
has finished this chapter, as I hope he will do, I think
he will agree that the only alternative to a thorough
study was an extremely summary account, and that
the latter would be of relatively little use, and might
well give rise to false impressions.

The artificial control of American cotton supplies did
not begin until 1929, but in order to understand why
and how the United States Government was induced
to initiate such control, it is essential to take note of
certain previous developments which are most relevant.
In point of time, the first of such developments was
the foundation of co-operative marketing organisations
among the cotton growers. Attempts to improve the
methods by which the growers sold their crops in the
primary markets and the general conditions of primary
marketing, date back far into the last century, but it
was not until after the war that co-operative societies
on modern lines, and using methods based on the
experience of the Californian fruit growers and other
agricultural producers, began to be established. The
difficulties and the drawbacks of the ordinary methods
of marketing by individual growers have already been
described, and the co-operative societies were established in the belief that collective marketing by the
growers in each district would bring about a great
improvement from the seller's point of view. It was
argued that if the growers in a district would make over

their crop to a co-operative association, the association could arrange for the cotton to be warehoused, financed and insured in a proper manner, and could then sell it gradually over the season at the most favourable times, while by grading the crop scientifically, higher prices would be got for the finer grades, thus rewarding the skilful grower in a way which rarely occurred under the unscientific "hog-round" system of selling. The co-operative associations also had in view the economies which might be obtained by centralised buying of machinery, seeds and so on, but improvement on the selling side was their primary object. The methods adopted by the different co-operative associations varied greatly, but as a generalisation it may be said that each grower had to bind himself, for periods sometimes up to five years, to dispatch the whole of his crops, after he had got the cotton ginned, to the head office of the co-operative association, and he would then draw an advance payment of 70–80 per cent., and sometimes more, of the estimated value of his crop at the current market price; the co-operative association would grade the cotton received from all the growers, and sell it either to spinners direct, or to exporters, or to large merchants, as and when it considered opportune; and when all the cotton of each grade was disposed of, the grower received a second and final payment according to the actual price obtained for the particular grade into which his cotton had been classed.

Now undoubtedly such methods of marketing offer great advantages to the grower, provided that the actual selling is performed with reasonable skill and efficiency. But the whole business was new and untried, while the cotton growers were conservative to an even more extreme degree than are most farmers, and so in the main they waited to join until the new organisations had proved their worth, a matter which was all the more difficult the fewer were the members. Again, many, when they became convinced and desired to join, found it virtually impossible to do so because their crops had been pledged in advance as security for loans from storekeepers and merchants. Again, the co-operative associations found it difficult to get honest and skilled organisers and officials, and the task of organising innumerable small growers over very large areas was most formidable. And so for these and other reasons the movement made relatively slow progress, and by 1929 only about one-tenth of the American crop was being marketed co-operatively.

The next development, which is specially relevant, was the introduction into Congress of the famous, or infamous, McNary-Haugen Bill in 1927. By that year, general opinion in the United States was becoming deeply concerned about the relative poverty of the cotton belt, and indeed of agricultural producers in general, especially in comparison with the ever-increasing prosperity of the industrial areas of the country. Part at least of that prosperity was due to the policy of high tariffs, and that was obviously not to the advantage of the exporters of wheat and cotton. Again, in 1926–27 it was commonly believed that manufacturing industry had been completely cured of the old tendency to alternations between boom and slump, and yet the trouble of good and bad harvests, and especially in cotton growing of high and low prices, had not been attacked in any way. The McNary-Haugen Bill was an attempt to remedy this feature of the agricultural situation, not only as regards wheat, though that was probably its primary objective, but also as regards cotton and other products. When there was a bumper crop, the surplus was to be bought by the Federal Government, and held until selling conditions improved; if loss was unavoidable, the loss was to be spread in some way over the industry as a whole. This Bill was never passed, but it did focus attention on the whole question of helping the farmer, and President Hoover returned from his re-election in 1928 pledged to do something for agriculture, and in particular for cotton as much as for wheat. The result was the Agricultural Marketing Act of 1929, and the establishment of the Federal Farm Relief Board.

This Board was provided with a relatively large sum of money, and virtually told to help farmers in whatever way it thought best. But so far as cotton was concerned, the first need was some machinery by which the Board could be brought into contact with the million or so growers whom it desired to help. The only existing organisations among the growers were the co-operative associations, and they only covered the producers of about 10 per cent. of the crop. However they were at least a nucleus, and so the Board arranged for the formation of a central organisation of all the local co-operative societies, which was called the American Cotton Co-operative Association. By this time the middle of October 1929 had been reached, and the price of cotton was declining heavily, but at any rate, according to the diagnosis of the Farm Board, this was due not to the size of the crop then being picked, though it was admittedly on the large side, nor to the Wall Street storm which, though imminent, had not yet burst, but simply to the fact that the weather had resulted in very early and rapid picking, and more cotton was being pressed on to the market than it could conveniently absorb. In other words, the price fall was a purely seasonal movement, and the very thing which orderly marketing could relieve, and in future avoid. Here was an obvious case where the Federal Farm Relief Board could justify its creation, and use its funds in a sound and legitimate way. So the Board announced that it would finance the co-operative associations to make advance payments to their members up to 16 cents, the market price being about 18 cents. This at once checked the fall in the price, and even though Wall Street crashed a few days afterwards, and the prices of most primary products crashed down like the prices of securities, the price of cotton kept up fairly well until the end of January 1930. Then it suddenly fell by 6 cents a pound, presumably because holders of stocks realised that the slump in business activity was more serious than they had hitherto supposed, and realised this suddenly and with one accord, as often happens under such circumstances in highly organised speculative markets. Among these holders of stocks were the co-operative associations, and it now came out that instead of holding the actual cotton which they had received from their members, and were supposed to have refrained from selling, they had in fact sold large quantities of this actual cotton, but at the same time had bought "futures"—that is, they had undertaken contracts to buy cotton at an agreed price in the future, mainly about four to six months ahead, i.e. in May, June and July 1934. These future contracts were undertaken in the expectation that by the date of delivery the price of cotton would have recovered, and so they would make a profit on these future contracts, which would offset the losses which they were incurring by selling their holdings of actual cotton. The trouble was, that with this heavy fall in the price of cotton, the co-operatives had to put up increased deposits with the brokers concerned in the usual way, so that, if the buyer ultimately defaulted, the contract could be cancelled by the broker paying to the seller the difference between the current market price and the price at which the buyer contracted to deliver; and many of the co-operative associations had no money to meet these now large differences.

Whether the Federal Farm Relief Board knew what the co-operatives had been doing, is to my knowledge uncertain, but the Board was now faced with a real dilemma: either it had to furnish the co-operative associations with the requisite funds, or it had to see the co-operative associations bankrupted, the money already loaned to them lost, and the disappearance of the only machinery through which it could discharge its duty of helping the growers. The Board inevitably chose the former alternative, and thereby took the first step into what was to prove a terrible quagmire.

So the Federal Farm Relief Board made itself responsible for the differences required on the future contracts, by which the co-operative associations had agreed to buy cotton in three or four months' time. Now in future contracts the parties are really speculating on the price-level which will rule in the future as compared with the price-level at the time the contract is made, and so when the time for fulfilling the contract arrives, the buyer usually allows the seller to settle the contract by paying the difference between the market price and the price in the contract. But the buyer can always insist on the seller delivering actual cotton, and this is what the co-operative associations did with their future contracts, now presumably under the orders of the Federal Farm Board. The result was that at the end of June the co-operative associations held about 1·3 million bales of actual cotton. Almost the whole of this stock was then taken over by a body established for the purpose, called the Cotton Stabilisation Corporation. All told, the stocks of the 1929 crop carried over into the crop year 1930–31 amounted to over 6 million bales, of which nearly 1·3 million were really held by the United States Government.

We come now to the 1930–31 crop. This crop proved to be about average, but the rapid contraction in the demand made a further accumulation of stocks inevitable. The Federal Farm Board in August 1930 promised to assist the co-operative associations to make an advance payment to the growers of 90 per cent. of the current value of their cotton. In an effort to prevent too drastic a fall in the price, the co-operative associations did not sell the whole crop during the season, and on July 1st, 1931, they held 2·1 million bales of actual cotton or future contracts to buy, which with the 1·3 million bales of the 1929 crop held by the Stabilisation Corporation made a total government holding of 3·4 million bales out of a total carry-over of 8·8 million bales. As regards consumption, this season was to prove the worst: over the season 1930–31 it failed to reach 11 million bales as compared with 15 million bales in 1928–29. But the lowest level of prices and the highest level of surplus stocks were to be reached in the next season.

For in 1931–32, though consumption was considerably larger, good weather produced a bumper crop of 16·6 million bales, for despite the most vigorous exhortations of the Federal Farm Board, there had been little reduction in the acreage sown. The Federal Farm Board in this season appears to have realised that, to adapt a vulgar phrase, it had bitten off all and possibly more than it could chew. Consequently the Board's main efforts were confined to persuading and cajoling the banks that the Government had done, and was still doing, its share, and that now it was the turn of the banks to undertake a national duty by providing finance for such part of the current crop as could not be sold without provoking a complete collapse in the price. The banks responded, and made loans for longish periods on about 3·5 million bales, i.e. on as much as the Government was itself already carrying. All told, the carry-over on July 1st, 1932, was no less than 12·8 bales, or rather more than a year's requirements at the current rate of consumption. The average price over the season was only 4·8d. as compared with 5·7d. in 1930–81 and 10·5d. in 1928–29.

During the season 1932–33 the situation was eased by a continued recovery in consumption and a crop rather below the average yield. Over the season, there was a small reduction of stocks and an appreciable improvement in the price. In the autumn of 1932 President Roosevelt was elected to succeed President Hoover, and during the interval before he took office in March 1933, various schemes for solving the cotton problem were put forward, and discussed in and outside Congress. But nothing was done, and the Federal Farm Board and the Stabilisation Corporation still continued to hold a total of about 3 million bales, for though large amounts were given to the Red Cross Society, nearly as much new cotton was acquired as security against loans made to the growers by the Federal Farm Board for the purchase of seed. Then, in March, President Roosevelt came into office, and as soon as he had dealt with the great banking crisis, the agricultural problem was tackled in a way as vigorous as it was daring. The general policy of the new Government, as embodied in the Agricultural Adjustment Act, was to raise the prices of basic products, such as wheat, cotton, maize, hogs, tobacco, etc., to their average levels during the five years 1909–14, and the Secretary of Agriculture was given the widest possible powers to achieve this object, including the power to levy process taxes on the consumption of these commodities by manufacturers, and to use the proceeds in order to provide for rental or benefit payments to producers who reduced their acreage under these crops, or in other ways reduced their production.

The Agricultural Adjustment Act was not finally passed until June 1933, and by then the whole of the 1933 cotton crop had been sown. But there was no thought of waiting for another year, and so the idea of paying growers to refrain from sowing so much cotton was transmuted into the idea of paying them to plough-in a proportion of the acreage already sown. At the same time, the opportunity was taken to free the new Government from the commitments of the Federal Farm Board which it had of course inherited, and this was done in a highly ingenious way. The growers were invited to make contracts with the Government by which they agreed to plough-in a part of the cotton acreage which they had already sown, and the Government in return offered them the following terms:

(a) the right to purchase government stocks of cotton at 6 cents per lb. to the extent of the estimated reduction of their own crop as the result of the ploughing-in;

and (*b*) in addition a payment per acre ploughed-in, varying from 6–12 dollars according to the average yield of the land;

or (*c*) if the grower did not choose to purchase government cotton under (*a*), the payment under (*b*) might rise to 20 dollars per acre.

The funds for these payments were to be provided by levying a process tax on cotton spinners equivalent to 4 cents per lb. of raw cotton.

Such in outline was the scheme for dealing with the 1933–34 cotton crop. In the end, the growers of 60 per cent. of the total crop chose to buy government cotton, and the amount so bought was roughly equal to the total stocks which the Government was carrying. The Roosevelt administration thus transferred at one stroke its inherited future liabilities back on to the growers, and cut the whole loss of the Federal Farm Board's operations to date. This loss was enormous: most of the cotton had probably been bought at anything between 12 and 15 cents, and costs of storage and interest charges for nearly three years must also be added: against this, the Government received 6 cents: and it is probable that the total loss was in the neighbourhood of £20 million.

The result of the ploughing-in contracts was the abandonment of no less than 10·4 million acres, which meant that the crop would have been about 4·5 million bales more than it actually was. But again the weather took a hand, and even from the reduced acreage no less than 13 million bales were produced, that is very little below the average of previous crops. By October 1933 the Government felt that further action was required, and so it took the still bolder step of promising to advance 10 cents per lb. not only on the current crop, but also on the cotton of previous crops which the growers had taken over as part of their compensation for ploughing-in. The current market price was 8·6 cents, and the Government was therefore making it possible for all holders of cotton to refrain from selling until the market price had risen to 10 cents, and really in practice much above that: in short the Government decided to force up the price to a much higher and purely artificial level. The result was that the market price rose rapidly to over 12 cents by February 1934, though in April and May there was some decline.

So far as the price is concerned, after May much depends on the progress of the growing crop. But before we come to that, we must consider what arrangements had been made as regards the acreage to be sown. For the 1934 crop, the Government offered to lease between 35 and 45 per cent. of each grower's cotton acreage, and to pay as rental $4\frac{1}{2}$ cents per lb. of the estimated production of the land so leased. Though the land was actually to be leased to the Government, the owner might use it for growing crops for his own consumption, or any crops not scheduled under the Agricultural Adjustment Act. Eventually over one million of these individual contracts were made with cotton growers, and all but 4 million acres, out of the total of 28 million acres actually sown, came under the scheme. The average reduction was 38 per cent., and the amount paid in compensation was well over 100,000 dollars, or say £20 million. And in view of this heavy cost involved to the users of cotton through the process tax, and to the nation generally, the Government felt that it would be unreasonable not to take every precaution to ensure that the object of all this expenditure, namely, a corresponding reduction in the crop, should be achieved. But especially after the experience of the bumper yields of 1933, it was clear that mere reduction of acreage was no solid guarantee of a correspondingly smaller crop, for it was no guarantee as to the weather, while in any case the growers might intensify their cultivation of the reduced area by using more labour and more fertilisers, and so obtain a larger yield. Incidentally, it seemed very unfair that the small minority of the producers, who had not come into the Government's scheme, should perhaps benefit more than those who had done so. Limitation of the crop to a total such as the reduced acreage might be expected to provide on the basis of a normal yield per acre, would ensure that neither the weather nor more intensive cultivation should waste the public money which was being poured out so liberally, while it would duly defeat and punish those who had not co-operated with the Government's scheme for acreage reduction. The Bankhead Act was therefore superimposed on the previous legislation in the early spring of 1934. This act limited the 1934–35 crop to 10·5 million bales by allotting individual sale

quotas to each grower, and placing a prohibitive tax on
all cotton offered for sale in excess of such quotas.

   With the prospect of a total carry-over of less than
11 million bales, with the current price at over 12 cents,
and with the virtual certainty that the coming crop
would not exceed 10·5 million bales, the Secretary of
Agriculture may well have felt in June 1934 that a.
great improvement had been effected in the general
cotton situation during the twelve months since the
Agricultural Adjustment Act had been placed on the
Statute Book. Actually his work was to prove even
more satisfactory than he had designed. For the
weather, realising that any goodness on its part had
been definitely frustrated by the Bankhead Act, turned
nasty, and attacked the growing crop with excessive
heat, drought and dust storms. The result was that
the 1934 crop failed by nearly one million bales to
reach the limit of 10·5 million bales allowed by the
Bankhead Act. While the thermometer soared upwards
in July and August 1934, cotton prices followed it,
and though there was some decline during the spring
of 1935, a general level of around 7*d.* or 12–13 cents
was maintained until August. But the whole credit
or blame for this cannot be placed on the weather.
Following the lines of his successful coup in 1933, the
Secretary of Agriculture decided in September 1934 to
make the most of his good fortune by advancing 12
cents per lb. on the current crop, which virtually
stabilised the price at the existing high level. At any
rate consumers thought it a high level, for during the

season 1934–35 the world bought steadily less and less American cotton. As against a consumption of over 14 million bales of American cotton in 1932–33, and 13·5 million bales in 1933–34, the world consumed only about 11·5 million bales in 1934–35. But with a crop of only 9·7 million bales, stocks were still substantially reduced. The total carry-over on August 1st, 1935, was about 8·8 million bales, as compared with 10·7 million bales in 1934; of the 1935 total the Government is said to hold nearly 6 million bales.

The size of the 1935–36 crop was fixed in January 1935 by the Secretary of Agriculture at 11 million bales, but it seems likely to be appreciably in excess of that figure. As regards the financing of the crop, the growers and their political representatives wanted a continuation of the 12 cent loan of the previous season, but the President's advisers were frightened lest the artificial maintenance of the market price at this level might restrict the exports of American cotton and encourage cotton growing in other countries, and they therefore desired a substantial reduction in the loan. Eventually at the end of August a compromise was reached. Loans are to be made by the Agricultural Adjustment Administration on the basis of only 9 cents per lb., but the growers are to be guaranteed a price of 12 cents, the Administration making deficiency payments to them if the market price falls below 12 cents. This promptly happened, and during September the price was under 11 cents. Thus the general arrangements for the 1935–36 crop are now settled, but after this season anything may happen; no one can foretell how they will work out, and though in July the Senate authorised the extension of the Bankhead Act for another two years, several district courts have decided that it contravenes the constitution, and in due course the Supreme Court will make a final decision.

It is indeed impossible at present to see the end of this vast series of experiments in artificial control. But attention may be drawn to certain general results and tendencies to date. In the first place it is clear that the Government's immediate objectives have been achieved to a very considerable extent. The price of cotton has been doubled, and raised by more than half the extent required to bring it up to the full 15 per cent. level at which the Government is said to be aiming. As a result, despite the reduction in acreage, the income of the cotton growers has been raised from an estimated total of $484 million in 1932 to $756 million in 1934, and to compensate for the reduction in acreage they have received in 1934 well over $100 million in addition. The consequent change in the whole economic conditions in the cotton belt is something which must not be under-estimated. But neither must the debit side of the account. In the first place the process tax has hit the cotton manufacturers as well as the consumer, for it is fairly certain that the former have not been able to pass on the whole of it to the consumer. Secondly there is the effect of the rise in the price of raw cotton on the domestic consumption, quite apart from the additional effects of the process tax: the demand for cotton goods is unquestionably very sensitive to price changes, and the growers of raw cotton have not been, and will not in the future be able to sell, even in the domestic market, anything like the total quantity of cotton at a price-level of 12–13 cents which they could do at several cents lower. Thirdly, and most important of all, there is the effect on the foreign demand for American cotton. This demand is, of course, even more sensitive to price changes because, within limits, foreign manufacturers can buy other kinds of cotton if American cotton becomes relatively dear. This they have in fact been doing on a scale which few people would have thought possible in the past. Outside the United States, consumption of other kinds of cotton has been rapidly increasing during the last three years, while the consumption of American cotton has been barely stationary. In the year ending July 31st, 1935, the world consumption of American cotton (i.e. including American domestic consumption) *decreased* by over one million bales, while the consumption of other kinds of cotton *increased* by nearly 1·5 million bales. The success of the American control schemes in raising the price has thus enabled cotton producers in other countries to expand their output considerably, and virtually new cotton exporting industries have been established, notably in Brazil. The expansion of cotton growing in these other countries may take several more years before it reaches a point which is really dangerous from the American point of view, and during that time the American Government may be able to hold prices at the present level, though even this is going to be extremely difficult. But if the present policy is pursued for more than a limited period, the export trade in American cotton will unquestionably be ruined. The alternative is to allow prices to decline to a much more reasonable level, but, if this happens, the growers in a large part of the south-eastern states will be brought once more to the verge of destitution. The only solution is to introduce into these states some other crop, or some generally diversified system of farming, in place of cotton growing, but it is a solution so difficult as to seem impossible, as all who know these states realise only too well. The cotton problem is indeed about the hardest of the many hard problems with which the United States is wrestling.

Postscript, December 14th, 1935. Since September, the price of American cotton has risen again to a 12 cent level, primarily because the 1935–36 crop is considerably smaller than was estimated in the summer, but partly also because the demand for American cotton shows some improvement. The 1935–36 crop is now estimated at only 10·7 million bales, and some further reduction of stocks should therefore occur during the present season, provided there is no decline in the demand. The Agricultural Adjustment Administration has just put forward a plan for controlling production for another four years: details are not yet available, but the 1936 crop is apparently to be limited to 11·5 million bales.

Chapter VI

CONTROL SCHEMES IN RUBBER

THE reader, who has accompanied the author thus far, may feel with him that a little relaxation from more ordinary and prosaic methods of study would not come amiss. Let us therefore take a short holiday tour in Malaya and the Dutch East Indies, and see for ourselves at first hand what rubber production and rubber producers are like. We shall return, I hope, not only sufficiently refreshed to make a serious study of the rubber industry and its problems, but also equipped with a considerable amount of very useful background knowledge.

We will go straight to Kuala Lumpur in the middle of the Malay Peninsula: it is marked on the map opposite just under the word Malaya. It is quite a considerable town, for it is the headquarters of the Government of the Federated Malay States, and also a big business centre as the capital of the world's most important rubber-producing area. It is now about 5 o'clock in the morning, and after a rather hot night, we are getting up, while it is still dark, in order to go in a car to the rubber estate of the X.Y.Z. Company, one of whose directors in London has kindly given us an introduction to their plantation manager. We drive off. The air is most refreshing, but if you want to, you may now continue your interrupted sleep, because it is

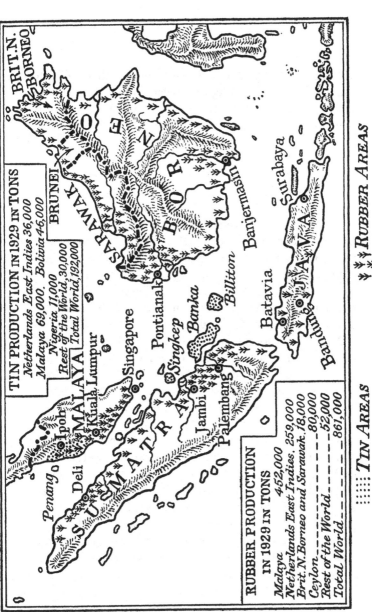

TIN PRODUCTION IN 1929 IN TONS

Netherlands East Indies 36,000
Malaya 69,000. Bolivia 46,000
Nigeria 11,000
Rest of the World, 30,000
Total World,192,000

RUBBER PRODUCTION
IN 1929 IN TONS

Malaya   452,000
Netherlands East Indies. 259,000
Brit.N.Borneo and Sarawak.18,000
Ceylon------80,000
Rest of the World------52,000
Total World------861,000

::::: *TIN AREAS*   ⁂ *RUBBER AREAS*

THE EAST INDIES: RUBBER AND TIN AREAS

still dark and you cannot see much, although the eastern sky is getting lighter every moment. If you do keep awake, you will see before long that our road is becoming lined with thick belts of trees 20–30 feet high, and planted in regular lines at such a distance that they just about touch each other. Very soon we arrive at a bungalow. The manager comes out to meet us, and we all set off walking under the trees on a tour of the estate.

It is now half light, and we shall probably realise very soon that we are not the only people about, even at this early hour. Little parties of twos and threes and fours are moving off in different directions, and gradually splitting up. These are the tappers going out to their particular sections of the estate. Every moment it is getting lighter, and at a much greater speed than we are accustomed to in England.

Now let us look at the trunk of one of these innumerable trees. The first four feet or so from the ground are neatly divided by scoring the bark into two or three sections or panels, and at the top of one of these panels we see that the bark has been removed quite recently. In another panel, on the other side of the tree, the bark has also been removed, but it is now growing again. Here comes one of the tappers, and we will watch what he is going to do. By the way, note that he is not a Malay, but an Indian. He walks up to the tree, and with a barrel-shaped knife he slices off a strip of bark about $\frac{1}{4}$ inch wide from the lower edge of the bare patch: in other words, the patch is now just a very little bigger. Almost at once we see a white liquid, like milk, oozing out from where he has just removed the bark. He then adjusts the position of a little metal spout stuck into the tree so that it will catch this "milk" as it runs downwards—for the cut is made in a sloping direction towards the ground—and so that its dripping is directed into a little cup which he puts below it or on the ground at the foot of the tree.[1] And then he goes to the next tree. It is all done very quickly and neatly, and it needs to be, because he has to do about two hundred trees before 9 or 10 o'clock. After that time it begins to get so hot that the "milk" will not ooze to anything like the same extent. The earlier the tapping is done in the morning, the bigger the yield, and that is why tapping begins the moment it is light enough to see, and why we have had to make such an early start.

What I have referred to as "milk" is, of course, the rubber, and you will appreciate now that the yield of rubber per tree depends upon the extent of bark on the trunk. By heavy tapping, that is, by cutting large slices of bark continuously every day, you can get a big yield for a short time, but when you have cut off all the bark, you will not be able to get any more until the bark has grown again, and that will take some four to six years depending on the vitality of the tree and many other things. Now, the policy of most European estates is to obtain a steady permanent yield by tapping just as fast as the bark renews itself, and no faster. The skilful manager concentrates on getting maximum

[1] See illustration facing page 128.

yield with minimum bark consumption, and with the quickest possible bark renewal; hence very elaborate systems of periodical tapping and periodical resting of the trees have been evolved, and considerable care is devoted to keeping the trees in the best possible condition by proper drainage systems, treatment of disease and so on.

The manager will have many things to show us, and much to tell us, but, with one exception, I must not stop to describe them or attempt to repeat what he is saying. The one exception must be just a word about his patch of budded trees. Individual rubber trees vary greatly in yield, but the trouble is that a high-yielding tree does not necessarily transmit its good qualities to the seed which it produces. Until only a few years ago estates were planted from seed. Some trouble was taken to get a good strain of seed, but even so the yield per acre would be an average of high-yielding trees and low-yielding trees, and the range of yields would be very large. Lately, science has been applied to the selective breeding of rubber trees, and propagation now takes place by budding the shoots of the very best trees on to suitable root stocks, just in the same sort of way as roses are budded on to briar stocks. A rough average of the yield of all the more recently established estates would be round about 400 lb. of rubber per acre per year: on especially good estates it might average 600 lb.; but it is now possible to plant budded stock which will give with certainty a yield of at least 1000 lb. per acre. I want you just to bear this point in mind; it will come in useful on our return home.

Of course, in normal times we should see a lot of other work going on besides the tapping—weeding, draining and the general upkeep of the estate—but with the low prices of the last few years all this work has been cut to a minimum. After our tour of the estate, we shall almost certainly be entertained to breakfast by the manager—for rubber managers are a hospitable crowd—and after that he will probably take us to visit the factory. When the trees have ceased oozing, the tappers collect the cups and pour them into big cans, which are collected by lorry from central points on the estate, and taken to the factory. Here the "milk", or latex as it is called, is strained to remove any dirt, and put into large shallow tanks. Certain chemicals are then stirred into the tanks which solidify the liquid in quite a short time. The result is large slabs of pale-looking rubber, something like the *crêpe* rubber used for boots. These slabs are then rolled out by power-driven machinery into thin sheets with a ribbed marking, and taken to the smoke house. A thorough smoking alters the colour to a rich brown, and we now have the standard product, ribbed smoked sheet. The sheets are about 36 inches long by 12 inches wide, and they are then packed into plywood cases, and dispatched to the railhead and from there to the ports, and so to Europe or the United States of America.

After seeing the factory, we shall probably walk round the village where the labourers live. Most

British estates recruit their labour from villages in Southern India. The length of terms of service, the minimum rate of pay, and many other conditions, are fixed by agreement between the Government of India and that of the Malay States. Usually the Indian workers go back to India at the end of their contract period, but a large percentage return regularly, and often return with their wives. They spend the bulk of their lives in Malaya, for they can get a much higher standard of living there than in India, but they usually return to India for a visit every now and then.

That is the sort of thing you will find on the typical European-owned estates in Malaya, Ceylon or the Dutch East Indies. It is essentially a capitalistic method of production. The whole thing is very well organised. Considerable use is made of scientific knowledge, and the policy as regards production is based on the long view rather than the short. The size of estates varies enormously, the most common being about 2000 acres.

Now, as well as these European-owned estates, there are considerable numbers of Chinese-owned estates in Malaya. These, as a rule, run rather smaller, but they have the same characteristics as the European-owned estates, only in a lesser degree: for example, a Chinese estate is usually planted with more trees to the acre, is usually tapped more severely in times of high prices, and so on. There is, in general, less organisation and less application of science.

So then we have European estates and Chinese estates, but in Malaya there is also a large production

Tapping a rubber tree

A European rubber estate

A "native" rubber holding

of rubber by Malay natives, owning small holdings up
to five acres in extent. Here the whole conditions are
very different. The Malay native nowadays wants some
cash wherewith to buy manufactures, if he can possibly
get it. Practically speaking, the only way he can get it
is by producing and selling rubber; and so part or even
the whole of his land is planted with rubber trees.
He plants them very close together,[1] and taps them
often heavily and always carelessly, at least as judged
by European standards, but all the same he gets very
high yields for considerable periods at a time, because
the rubber tree will stand a great deal of rough usage,
if it gets a periodical rest; and in general, when the
price of rubber is high, the Malay native taps less,
because he has no keen ambition to grow rich, and when
he has got a certain income, he prefers leisure to work;
thus, in times of high prices his trees generally get some
rest, while his methods of planting and cultivation,
though disadvantageous in some respects, do result in
a rapid renewal of bark. The native and his family
normally do all the work, and it must be understood
that he has no capital charges. He prepares his rubber
by very simple methods. He solidifies the latex in four-
gallon petrol tins cut in halves, and rolls out the slabs
roughly in hand machines much like our home mangles.
Sometimes he smokes the sheets, but very often he sells
his rubber unsmoked to the Chinese dealers. It does
not fetch as good a price as the product of European
estates, but it costs very little to produce. And please

[1] Compare the illustrations facing this page.

note that the Malay native does not usually increase his output in times of high prices, while, on the other hand, if prices are very low, he produces as much as he possibly can in order to get at least some cash.

What I have just been saying concerns the production by natives in Malaya; in Sumatra, Borneo and certain other islands of the Dutch East Indies, the natives also produce rubber, but in very different conditions from those in Malaya. Sumatra is in general thinly populated, and since there is plenty of land, the natives do not settle down permanently and cultivate the same piece of land year after year as they do in Malaya. Every year the Dutch native clears about two acres of forest land in order to grow rice, which is his staple food. After one crop, or at the most two, he abandons this clearing, and makes another, moving his hut when necessary: the abandoned clearing simply reverts to jungle. But during the last fifteen or twenty years, these Dutch natives have gradually learned about rubber, and more and more it became the practice to plant the area to be abandoned with rubber, by the simple process of pushing rubber seeds into the ground with the thumb when he planted his rice crop, or as soon as the rice crop was cleared. If the young rubber trees are to survive, the native must keep down the growth of weeds for the first three or four years: after that the trees are tall enough to take care of themselves. Especially in 1925 and 1926, when the price of rubber was extremely high, an enormous amount of this planting of what are really "rubber forests" took place.

To the Dutch native, therefore, rubber is essentially a by-product of his normal agricultural operations. If the price of rubber is high enough to make it worth his while to tap, or to hire assistants to do the tapping, the Dutch native will produce rubber; if all the planted area were being tapped, the total production to-day would be very large; but when the price of rubber is low, it ceases to be worth his while to tap, for in general the Dutch native has not yet developed the insistent need for manufactures, and consequently the need for cash wherewith to buy them, to anything like the extent to which the natives in Malaya have done. Apart from this, however, if the price of rubber falls very low—say to 2d. or less, as it has done recently— a large proportion of the natives find that they cannot sell their rubber at all, because the price will not cover the costs of transport to the big markets, and of course when this happens, they are forced to stop tapping altogether. In Malaya this does not happen to the same extent, for the majority of Malay small-holdings are within fairly easy reach of a market. Thus the reaction of the Dutch native and the native in Malaya to changes in the price of rubber are very different.

These, then, are the main kinds of rubber producers. Now, as we travel home, I will try and give you some idea of their relative importance at different times. None of them was in existence as a producer in 1900. At that time there was no production of rubber in the East. Practically the whole of the world's supply of rubber at that time came from the Amazon Valley and

Central Africa, where rubber trees grew wild in the forests, and expeditions were organised to travel round and tap them. Round about 1900 the first commercial planting of rubber in Malaya began. Now, from this date also begins the rapid growth of the motor-car industry with its demand for rubber for tyres. The price of rubber began to rise very steeply, and in 1909 and 1910 there was the first great price boom when rubber touched 12s. per lb. and averaged nearly 9s. for the whole of 1910. The total world production in that year consisted of 83,000 tons of wild rubber from the Amazon and Africa, and 11,000 tons of plantation rubber from the East. These high prices led to the rapid planting up of estates in Malaya, Ceylon and Java. By 1914, 2½ million acres had been planted, but it must not be forgotten that it takes six or seven years for the trees to grow to a size when they can be tapped. Planting by Chinese, by natives in Malaya, and, to a small extent, by Dutch natives also began. It was clear that a hugely increased production would take place when all this new planting came into bearing, but meantime the total plantation production was only between 70,000 and 80,000 tons, and the price remained as high as 2s.

During the war the great trouble in the rubber industry was the shortage of shipping. In 1917 rubber was selling in Singapore at half the price it was fetching in London, simply because it could not be transported. Stocks were piled up in Malaya, and a voluntary restriction scheme was introduced. In 1919 no less than

350,000 tons were exported from the East, and though probably 50,000 of that represented accumulated stocks, the current production was certainly 300,000 tons a year, because all the pre-war plantings were now coming into bearing. The London price fluctuated round about 2s. In the middle of 1920 came the post-war slump in the United States, which was then consuming about two-thirds of the world's production of rubber. The United States manufacturers more or less stopped buying, and the price fell abruptly to 10d., at which level most estates could at that time barely cover their costs. Voluntary restriction of output was again tried under the auspices of the Rubber Growers' Association of London. But there was considerable opposition, and in 1921 some of the members of the Rubber Growers' Association fought against the renewal of the restriction scheme. The condition of an industry in which so much British capital was invested, and the consequent economic position of Malaya and Ceylon, now caused the British Government to intervene, and the famous Stevenson Committee was appointed. That Committee presented its report in May 1922. They estimated that production in 1922 would total 400,000 tons, and world consumption not more than 300,000 tons, and that on January 1st, 1922, surplus stocks, that is, over and above necessary stocks, had totalled 110,000 tons, which figure would therefore be doubled by the end of the year. The price meantime had fallen to about 8d. The Committee in its first report advised that no restriction scheme could be effective without the co-operation of the Dutch. Efforts were therefore made to persuade the Dutch Government to join, but without success. The Committee then reconsidered the situation, and eventually recommended the establishment of a restriction scheme by the British Government alone. Under the proposed scheme the price was to be stabilised at 1s. 3d. by varying the degree of restriction every quarter according to changes in the current price-level. If the price rose above 1s. 3d. the degree of restriction was automatically lessened: if the price fell below, it was automatically increased. The scheme was to start on November 1st, 1922, and would apply to Malaya and Ceylon.

Aided by the unexpectedly rapid recovery of consumption in the United States, all went well with the scheme for the first year. The initial restriction was to 60 per cent. of the estimated productive capacity, and the price jumped up considerably as soon as the scheme was published, and rapidly reached the desired figure. But during the first half of 1924, the price declined to an extent which resulted in an automatic tightening of restriction to 50 per cent. of the standard output. This brought about a quick recovery in the price, but it was really much more than a mere recovery. The world in general, and the United States manufacturers in particular, had been living in part on their stocks, which were now at a very low level. At the end of 1924 consumption in the United States took a sudden jump upwards, and heavy buying rapidly forced up the price. As the price rose higher and higher, the United States manufacturers rushed in to buy not merely their current requirements, but also their requirements for some time ahead. This rush to buy drove the price sky high to over 4*s.* in November 1925. The result was a large increase in the exports from countries outside the restriction scheme, mainly, of course, from the Netherlands East Indies, and also a big increase in the production of reclaimed rubber, that is, rubber recovered from worn-out tyres, etc. At the same time the United States Government appealed to the public to assist in breaking the British rubber monopoly by using their tyres as long as possible, repairing them instead of getting new ones, and so on. By the beginning of 1926 the full effects of these developments began to be felt. The price began to fall, while at the same time restriction was being automatically removed as the result of the high prices which were now becoming a thing of the past. By October 1926 the price was down to 1*s.* 9*d.*, and then the whole restriction scheme was revised in order to try and prevent the price falling below this figure. The previous standard of 1*s.* 3*d.* had been sufficiently profitable: the new standard meant enormous profits to all producers outside the scheme, and therefore a direct incentive to them to increase their output to the greatest possible extent, which they naturally did. Looking back, it is hard to conceive how such a blunder could ever have been made by a British Government. As fast as more and more restriction was reimposed on British areas in the effort to stop the price from falling, other countries, and chiefly, of course, the Dutch East Indies, increased their output, and the supply of rubber continued to be all, and more than all, the world required. The British restriction scheme was benefiting Malaya not at all, but her chief competitor very much. Throughout 1927 the price continued to fall, until restriction again reached 60 per cent. of the standard output, which under the new scheme was to be the minimum. Thereafter the price still continued to fall. Eventually, in March 1928, the British Government realised the blunder which had been committed, and it was decided that all restrictions on production should be removed as from the following November 1st, this long notice being given to enable British estates to arrange for the additional migration of labour from Southern India on the scale required for full production.

The outlook for 1929 seemed pretty black from the producers' point of view. Consumption was increasing, but it seemed most unlikely that it would increase sufficiently to absorb the enormous increase in ,production, seeing that in 1928 Malaya and Ceylon had been restricted to 60 per cent. of their full output. But in the end consumption exceeded all estimates. Production also did the same, but only ended the year some 60,000 tons ahead: this amount, however, could be easily absorbed into current stocks, which had been very low at the end of restriction. During the spring of 1929 the price rose to 1s., and even up to September it continued above 10d. But then the Wall Street crash checked American buying, and by the end of the year the price was down to 8*d*., that is, where it had been at the beginning.

Before the sad tale of 1930 is begun, mention must be made of one other event of 1929, namely the discovery that the average costs of estate production in Malaya were less than had been generally supposed. During the six years of restriction, the trees had not only had a good deal of rest from tapping, but they had been better cared for, and the methods of cultivation had been much improved, while better and cheaper systems of tapping had also been discovered. The effect on costs had been concealed while restriction was still in force, but when full production was resumed, it was realised that the total costs of production on average estates were between 6*d*. and 7*d*. per lb., and that therefore a price of only 9*d*.–10*d*. would suffice to give reasonable profits, instead of the 1*s*. which had been considered as an absolute minimum. This was a matter of vital importance for the future prospects of the estate industry. It was mentioned above that during the price boom of 1925 and 1926 there was an enormous amount of new planting by the Dutch natives in Sumatra and Borneo. These new plantings would become tappable by 1931, or 1932, and if the price was high enough to make it worth while to tap all these newly planted areas, it was estimated that the Dutch native rubber output would rapidly rise from the 100,000 tons produced in 1929 to 300,000 tons by, say, 1934, and subsequently even higher. This would mean a world production in 1934 perhaps as high as 1,300,000 tons, and even before the world depression appeared, it seemed most unlikely that consumption could increase to that extent. There was obviously going to be a struggle between the European estates and the Dutch natives as to which would be able to supply the world's requirements at the cheapest price, and therefore this decline in the costs of European estates was most welcome from their point of view, for the lower the price required for profitable production by the estates, the less the Dutch natives would find it worth while to produce.

So the year 1929 on the whole was not nearly so disastrous to the rubber industry as had been feared. But from the beginning of 1930 the situation rapidly changed for the worse. Buying by United States manufacturers continued to dwindle rapidly, surplus stocks began to accumulate, and by the summer of 1930 rubber producers realised that they had to face a genuine world depression, and not merely a temporary recession of business in the United States. The alarm spread rapidly, and there was soon talk of resurrecting restriction in some form or another. Arrangements were made by the Rubber Growers' Association for a stoppage of all tapping during the month of May 1930 on all British and Dutch estates. But this "tapping holiday", as it was called, was a hopelessly inadequate means of meeting the situation, and by mid-June the price was down to 6d. During the autumn of 1930, conversations on the subject of a possible restriction scheme took place between the Government of Malaya

and that of the Dutch East Indies. When these conversations were officially terminated by a public
announcement that neither government would interfere, and that economic forces must be allowed to run
their course, the price fell quickly to 4*d.* But despite
the fall in price, production did not decline very much,
while consumption went on diminishing, especially in
the United States during the summer of 1931. As a
result, British and Dutch producers again discussed
the question of restriction, and this for a time helped
to check the decline in the price. But eventually these
negotiations once more resulted in a joint conclusion
that restriction was impracticable. This definitely put
an end to any hopes of restriction in the near future,
and by September 1931 the price had fallen to 2½*d.* It
reached its lowest level at just over 1½*d.* in June 1932.
During the autumn of 1932 and the spring of 1933,
however, there was some recovery in consumption, and
early in 1933 negotiations concerning the possibilities
of restriction were once more restarted between the
British and Dutch growers. Under the combined influence of the increasing consumption and these renewed
possibilities of restriction, the price began to rise
rapidly, and in May 1933 reached about 3*d.*

The revival of restriction talks begins yet another
phase in this very complicated story, and before this
new phase is examined, it is desirable to obtain some
idea of the results of unrestricted production and low
prices on the various kinds of producers. World production in 1932 was roughly 130,000 tons less than in

1929, and the price in 1932 averaged $2\frac{1}{4}d.$ per lb., as compared with $10\frac{1}{4}d.$ in 1929. Seeing that the 1929 price was not especially profitable, one is really inclined at first sight to wonder that anything at all was produced at this 1932 price! Actually, estates in Malaya as a whole produced at about the same rate as in 1929, while the Dutch estates showed an even higher production in 1931, and about the same in 1932. It seems simply incredible perhaps, but the whole level of the 1929 costs of production was rapidly scaled down in three main ways. First of all, there were terrific reductions in salaries and wages. Secondly, all but absolutely essential maintenance and cultivation work was given up, and the number of men employed was reduced to a minimum. Thirdly, efficiency in general was increased under the spur of necessity, and certain newly discovered methods were introduced. It must be explained, however, that while some estates, which could afford it, restricted their output as the price fell, in order to conserve their bark against the time when tapping would be more profitable, other estates were driven to tap more severely than is normally desirable, in order to obtain the largest possible output over which to spread their overhead costs, and it was as the result of this balance that the total output of estates showed little change. By the end of 1932 a majority of Malayan companies had got their costs down to $3d.$ or even lower. But this would not include proper allowance for maintenance or amortisation, while it must be remembered that salaries and wages were at a bare subsistence

level. In other words, such low costs must not be regarded as a new level of proper normal costs: rather
they represented costs of production in an emergency,
and as such they could be maintained for perhaps two
or three years, but not permanently.

Nevertheless, from the point of view of the companies
this reduction of costs was a very fine achievement.
But there is another side of the picture. Hundreds of
British assistants and even managers had to be dismissed,
and thousands of wage earners were returned to India,
their contracts cancelled. Those who remained at work
were earning, at the end of 1932, rather less than half
what they were earning in 1929. The return of these
labourers to their homes in Southern India means for
them a poor subsistence level. The lot of the assistants
and managers has in a way been even worse. Many of
them stayed in the East, living on their savings and
hoping to find a job. When their savings were exhausted,
they had to fall back on what amounts to Poor Law
relief from the Government of Malaya. Thus the reduction of costs was a fine achievement from one point
of view, but the heavy price in human suffering must
not be overlooked.

So much for the estate industry. Now let us consider
the native producers in Malaya and the Dutch East
Indies. The former maintained their output during
1930 and 1931, but it dropped some 20,000 tons in 1932.
The Dutch native output, however, fell by nearly one-
half—from 108,000 tons in 1929 to 61,000 tons in 1932.
The Malay natives are mostly within fairly easy reach

of their markets, but a large proportion of the Dutch natives in the interior of Sumatra and Borneo simply could not find buyers, because the price of rubber at the big port markets would not cover the costs of transport from the interior. Moreover, the Dutch native grows his own foodstuffs, and can turn to the production of other crops much more easily than the Malay native, while his need for cash is less developed: consequently most of the Malay natives went on producing as long as they could get any price at all for their rubber, whereas it was only the Dutch natives near the ports who still found it possible to sell rubber, or at least to sell it at a price which seemed to them worth the labour involved. Thus, the effect of low prices on production was very different in the two cases. The combined decrease in native output accounts for half the decrease in the world output. Of the other 65,000 tons decrease, Ceylon produced 30,000 tons less, and most of the smaller countries also produced less.

So much for production, now just a word about consumption. In 1929 world consumption had been 807,000 tons: in 1931 and 1932 it was round about 680,000 tons. The whole decline was accounted for by the United States: consumption in Great Britain and in the rest of the world on balance remained the same as in 1929: a very remarkable fact. But mention must also be made of the fact that if there had not been a great decline in the use of *reclaimed* rubber in the United States, the world's consumption of *raw* rubber would probably have declined by another 70,000 tons. It was not worth while using reclaimed rubber at the 1932 price of crude rubber. But though consumption declined less than might have been expected, it, of course, declined much more rapidly and much further than production, with the result that by 1932 surplus stocks, over and above normal stocks, amounted to over 200,000 tons.

With these surplus stocks, with production still above consumption, even though consumption did seem to be increasing again at last, and with the virtual certainty that at any price above, say, 3*d*., the Malayan and Dutch natives would rapidly and greatly increase their output, and with the fact that at 3*d*. even the better European estates could barely make ends meet —it was under these circumstances that informal negotiations were once more resumed in the spring of 1933, as has been said, between the British and Dutch growers. And the Dutch Government now showed itself an interested party. The Netherlands East Indies, as a Dutch colony, has remained with Holland on the gold standard, and both home and colonial governments were finding it most difficult to balance their budgets. The new Dutch Prime Minister, who took office during 1933, was definitely favourable to restriction on the grounds, as he put it, that "new taxpayers must be created". The great difficulty was, of course, the native production. It was considered impossible to assess the native producers individually, and then regulate their output by a quota as is the usual practice with restriction schemes. It was impossible not only because of their numbers, but because much of their lands has never even been surveyed, and the general governmental control of the natives in the interior of Sumatra and Borneo is inevitably slender. Moreover, the Dutch were afraid that political trouble might follow too much interference in native affairs. All through 1933, however, and the opening months of 1934, negotiations went on, and eventually the difficulties and scruples of the Dutch were overcome, and, encouraged perhaps by the apparent success of the restriction schemes for tea and tin, they decided to take the plunge. In April 1934 it was announced that agreement had been reached between the British and Dutch Governments, and also Siam and French Indo-China, and that a scheme for the regulation of their exports of rubber would begin on June 1st, 1934.

The scheme is administered by the governments concerned and by the International Rubber Regulation Committee, consisting of representatives appointed by those governments, with voting power according to the production quotas assigned to the different countries. These production quotas are fixed on the basis of past exports, with allowances for recently planted areas not yet in full production: thus they increase every year as the newer areas become more mature, and newly planted areas become tappable. For example, the quota for Malaya in 1934 was fixed at 504,000 tons, rising to 602,000 tons in 1938. The Dutch East Indies quota was 352,000 tons for 1934 and 485,000 in 1938. The percentage of these quotas which the countries may export, is fixed from time to time by the Regulation Committee, and its first act was to fix the percentage at 100 per cent. (i.e. no restriction) for June and July 1934, 90 per cent. for August and September, 80 per cent. for October and November, and 70 per cent. for December. The Committee has complete power to impose whatever degree of restriction it thinks fit, in order to reduce existing world stocks to a normal figure and to maintain "a fair and equitable price-level which will be reasonably remunerative to efficient producers". The determination of what such a price-level is, rests with the Committee, though a body representing the world's manufacturers has also been established, which the Committee can consult. Such are the essential outlines of the scheme, but another important point is that new planting is prohibited, except for experimental purposes, while research is to be encouraged, and so on. The scheme is to last until the end of 1938.

Now, the effect of all these negotiations, coupled with a very considerable increase in consumption, had been to raise the price from 3d. in May 1933 to over 5d. in February and March 1934. The result was that the Dutch native output practically doubled, while the Malay native output, and the production of Ceylon and the smaller countries, rapidly rose. Until the beginning of restriction, everything on the production side followed the expectations of what would happen if the price rose to such levels. In the end both world pro-

duction and consumption in 1933 were roughly the
same as in 1929, but, as in 1929, production was the
greater by some 40,000 tons. When the expectations
of restriction were fulfilled in April 1934, the price rose
to 6*d.*, and in July, August and September to over 7*d.*
per lb.; after which it fell to a little over 6¼*d.* Production in 1934 just exceeded one million tons, an increase
of 150,000 tons over 1933, and no less than 300,000 as
compared with 1932. Consumption in 1934 was nearly
940,000 tons, an increase of 30,000 tons over 1933, and
no less than 250,000 tons as compared with 1932. Thus
despite restriction in the latter part of the year, and
despite the increase in consumption, a further 60,000
tons was added to the accumulated stocks. But the
matter of stocks requires a word of explanation. In
1931 and 1932, when consumption was so much reduced,
total stocks were equivalent to over 10 months' requirements, the necessary or convenient equivalent
being about six months'; but though the actual volume
of stocks was much greater at the end of 1934, yet,
owing to the great increase in consumption, its their
to consumption was only 8½ months; thus the true
surplus was really much smaller, though the actual
volume was greater.

During 1935 restriction has become really effective,
and production has been definitely below consumption.
For the first quarter of the year, the exportable percentage was raised from 70 to 75, and it was announced
that this would continue during the second quarter and
would be reduced to 70 per cent. for the third quarter.

But as the result of a sharp fall in the price during March, the Regulation Committee changed its mind, and ordained 70 per cent. for the second quarter and 65 per cent. for the third.[1] But though this fall in the price was occasioned directly by the pepper crisis, which unsettled nearly all commodity markets, it had a more solid basis in the failure of American consumption to maintain the considerable advance made during the previous December and January. World consumption for the first six months of 1935 was very disappointing and was somewhat lower than during the first half of 1934. On the other hand production was very considerably lower than in 1934, and the reduction of the surplus stocks has thus begun, though, even with the tightening of restriction in the second half of the year, it will be very small unless consumption greatly increases. Up to September 1935, the machinery of restriction has on the whole worked smoothly and efficiently. In some months exports from certain countries exceed their quotas, but in other months they fall short, and the total exports over the first year of restriction were under and not over the permissible total. The regulation of Dutch native production is in fact the only really difficult problem, for no system of individual quotas for each native producer could be introduced by the Government of the Dutch East Indies, though it is being attempted in certain districts, and so restriction of their native output took the form of imposing an export tax. This was originally fixed at about 3d. per lb.

[1] The percentage for the final quarter was 60.

During the first four months of the scheme (June–Sept. 1934) when the London price was over 7*d.*, the exports of Dutch native rubber were much in excess of their total quota, but during the latter months of 1934 when the London price dropped to under 6½*d.*, they fell far below it. Consequently in December 1934 the tax was reduced to a little under 2½*d.*, and during the first half of 1935, despite a fall in the price to below 6*d.*, native exports increased again, and were considerably, though not seriously, in excess of the quota. It may be observed that the proceeds of this tax are to be used by the Government for the benefit of the natives in the rubber areas, the idea being that native producers are to get the benefit of restriction in the form of public works and so on.

So far therefore all seems to be going reasonably well, though the extent of the reduction of stocks is not as great as it was hoped it might be a year ago, and some producers would like to see a much greater rise in the price than has yet taken place. What then can be said concerning the wisdom of instituting this new restriction scheme? The case in favour may be briefly summarised as follows. Few, if any, of the leaders of the industry regard artificial control as desirable in itself: as a general proposition, they would much prefer conditions of free competition. But those who have been active in resurrecting restriction would, I think, argue that in the rubber industry the situation under competition had become intolerable, and seemed likely to continue to be intolerable for an indefinite period. The situation was intolerable, because at a price of under, say, 3*d*., few, if any, estates could cover their full proper costs, and even if the higher-cost companies after a time ceased production altogether, the trees on their estates would still be there, and benefiting by the rest, and as soon as the price rose appreciably, they would resume tapping, or if they had gone bankrupt, someone would have bought up the estate for a mere song, and would be able to resume production with virtually no capital charges. Equally, though the Malay native output had declined, as soon as the price rose appreciably, it would rise again, and the same was true of the potentially much more important Dutch native output: the Dutch native output had not declined seriously until the price fell below 3*d*., and it might be expected to increase again if the price rose much above 3*d*., while at a price-level which would give some profits to European estates, say 6*d*. or thereabouts, the Dutch native output would certainly be very large, if indeed that price or a little more would not draw out almost the full possible supply, which as the result of the heavy planting during the price boom of 1925 and 1926 is now at least 300,000 tons: the total possible world supply is probably at least 1,300,000 tons, and consumption even to-day is running at less than one million tons, and a year ago, when the restriction scheme was decided upon, it was much less than that. The present situation, therefore, seemed desperate, and the outlook hopeless. Restriction would, at least, relieve the present strain: as to the future—well, I hope

I am not unfairly representing them if I say that the restrictionists felt that restriction could hardly make things much worse, and that, after all, something might turn up to save the situation, if by restriction they could keep their heads above water for a bit longer.

Now in comparing the case for restriction with the case against, the trouble is that the anti-restrictionist is mainly concerned with the effects of restriction in the future—in other words he begins more or less where the restrictionist leaves off. "Of course", says the anti-restrictionist, "the immediate results of restriction, provided you can enforce it, will be beneficial at least to the European estates, but what about the effects in the more distant future? Surely the fundamental problem with which the rubber industry is faced, is whether the future lies with estate production or with the native production—whether, in other words, European estates can produce more cheaply than the Dutch native, because if they cannot, the whole industry will pass into the hands of the natives, since there is virtually no physical limit to the amount of rubber which Sumatra and Borneo could produce. Before the revival of restriction talks began, and prices rose, the Dutch native production had fallen to nearly half what it was even in 1929, while very few European estates had been forced to stop production. As soon as the price of rubber rose, the Dutch natives resumed production on a scale far above that of 1929. By re-introducing restriction, all the advantages which the European estates had secured in their fight with the

Dutch natives were thrown away: all the painful process of reducing costs had been endured for nothing. Unless restriction is to be permanent, the battle between the estates and the Dutch native producers will have to be fought all over again."

Time alone will show whether the fears of the anti-restrictionist will be realised. Meantime the estate industry is in a relatively flourishing condition, and the question whether the interests of the Dutch natives are being best served by imposing restriction upon them, or whether they are being penalised for the benefit of European capitalists, is primarily a moral and not an economic issue.

Postscript, December 14th, 1935. Various developments have occurred since September. Early in October the price of rubber rose again to above 6*d.*, and during that month Dutch native exports were more than double the permitted amount, although the export tax was repeatedly increased, and by mid-November amounted to approximately $4\frac{1}{2}d$. Apparently the Dutch Government is unwilling to attempt further restriction of the native output, and so, in an effort to regularise the position, the International Committee has raised the Dutch East Indies quota for 1936 by 57,000 tons. The exportable percentage is to remain at 60 for the first six months of 1936. Meantime the Dutch are expediting their land surveys, in order to be able to introduce the individual quota system for their native producers in place of restriction by the export-tax method. The events of the last three months have thus emphasised, rather than diminished, the formidable nature of the problem of regulating Dutch native output.

Chapter VII

CONTROL SCHEMES IN TIN

TIN is a commodity of very special interest to students of artificial control because the present restriction scheme in the tin industry has been so successful that the price was more than doubled within two years, and for the last three years has stood at what would certainly be far above a reasonably profitable level if the producers were allowed to operate at full capacity. Indeed, it was mildly profitable, even when production was restricted to one-third of capacity. And yet, the outsider cannot perhaps help wondering whether it can be an aid to world recovery for consumers to have to pay such a high price for a staple raw material, and whether this policy can be really sound in the long run from the point of view of the industry. The history of the tin industry in recent years is therefore well worth studying.

As has just been said, the present price of tin is very high relatively to its cost of production; and yet the world does not seem to mind paying this price, and is certainly using more tin to-day than three or four years ago, when the price was half its present level. On the face of it this seems curious, but the situation becomes more intelligible if, for example, we consider the demand for tin by the motor industry. On the average about 5 lb. of tin are to-day used in the construction of a motor car. Now, if the price of tin is £300 per ton, the cost of this 5 lb. of tin will be about 9s. more than if the price of tin is £100 per ton! Therefore, whether more or less tin is used by the motor industry obviously depends primarily upon the price of motor cars, and the consequent demand for them, rather than directly on the price of tin. The producer of tin cannot increase his sales to the motor industry very much even if he cuts his price in half, while if the price is doubled, he will probably sell nearly as much, because there are no very good substitutes for tin, or perhaps I should say that it is hardly worth the motor manufacturer's while to discover them.

This situation arises from the fact that in the manufacture of motor cars, tin is used in small quantities in association with many other metals and raw materials, and this is generally speaking true of all the other uses of tin. The greatest single use for tin is, of course, in making tins, but tins are made not solely of tin, but of steel plate with a very thin coating of tin. The cost of tin matters, of course, very much more to the tin-plate manufacturer than to the motor manufacturer, but even so, it is not, for example, like the cost of raw cotton to the cotton spinner. And to most other users of tin, it matters hardly, if at all, more than to the motor manufacturer, because, as has been said, tin is used in very small amounts relatively to the value of the article produced. However, if the price of tin rises abnormally high, it is not long before business men realise that profits can be made by recovering tin from old metal junk heaps. Even with a normal price, this takes place to a small extent, for example with old motor-car radiators which contain a lot of tin in the solder, and the amount of recovered or "secondary" tin became very considerable during the high-price years of 1926 and 1927. The increased recovery of secondary tin thus tends to mitigate a shortage of new tin, though it is not a very effective means of checking the resulting high price. But a prolonged maintenance of very high prices for tin would almost certainly stimulate tin users to find substitutes, and in particular there is already a certain amount of competition between aluminium and tin.

The nature of the demand for tin is therefore one of the reasons why the price of tin fluctuates in so notorious a fashion. If production is only a little in excess of requirements, the price will fall severely, because consumption is not much increased as the price falls; and *vice versa*. The other reason is that the holding of stocks is a very costly business because tin is such a valuable metal—it means locking up a great deal of money to buy even a few hundred tons at say £150–£200 per ton. Consequently a fall in price is not usually checked by buying for stock-holding until that fall has gone a long way, and people expect a considerable and rapid increase to occur almost at once. The converse is equally true: if there is a slight shortage, there will be a very sharp rise in price. Finally, on the subject of consumption, it should be noted that Europe consumes roughly one-half of the world's production, and the United States the other half, though, as will now be shown, the United States neither produces nor even smelts a single ton, and is thus wholly dependent on other countries for its supplies of tin.

Turning to the production side, a glance at the statistics of world production printed in the map on page 123 shows that tin ore is relatively rare, and that it is distributed very irregularly over the world's surface. In 1929, the record year of production, the world's tin output was 192,000 tons. Of this, two-thirds came from one belt running diagonally down the south-east corner of Asia, beginning in Lower Burma, passing through Siam and Malaya, and appearing in three small islands in the Dutch East Indies—Banka, Billiton and Singkep—off the east coast of the southern half of Sumatra. There are also small deposits in Southern China and in French Indo-China. The most important of these Asiatic countries is Malaya which produced 69,000 tons, nearly twice as much as the Dutch East Indies. Altogether South-east Asia produced 126,000 tons. The next biggest source is right on the other side of the world, in Bolivia, which produced 46,000 tons, or say 25 per cent. of the world's total. Then midway, so to speak, between these two areas is the comparatively new Nigerian tin field which produced 11,000 tons. That leaves less than 4 per cent. of the total unaccounted for, and of that, about one-half came from Cornwall, Spain and Portugal, and the other half from Australia.

Tin is indeed a rare metal, and it shares a peculiarity

with two other rarer metals, gold and platinum, in that
it is found both in ordinary seams in solid rock, and
also in deposits of earth washed down by rivers and
water action generally. In Bolivia the tin is in underground seams, but in South-east Asia it is almost
entirely in deposits. Now these deposits can be worked
in a fairly simple fashion. The tin-bearing earth is
usually covered with a few feet of ordinary soil which
has to be stripped off, and then the tin-bearing earth
can be dug out by hand, mixed with water in a sump
at the bottom of the mine, and pumped up to the
highest point of a long inclined sluice box down which
the mixture of earth and water flows, the tin being
deposited along the bottom of the sluice box because
it is so much heavier than the earth. That is the general
method[1] by which the Chinese mine tin in Malaya
to-day. But just before the war European companies
were formed to get the tin by an entirely different
method, namely, by the use of dredges. A tin dredge
is really only a superior edition of the ordinary dredge
which one sees working in the harbours and rivers of
this country. A sufficiently large hole has to be dug,
and then filled with water to float the dredge. After
that the dredge puts down its long arm, and the buckets
begin going round bringing up the earth; the tin is then
separated on board, and when it has been taken out,
the earth is discharged over the tail of the dredge. Thus
the dredge[2] floats on a small artificially made lake which

[1] See upper illustration facing this page.
[2] See lower illustration facing this page.

An "open-cast" tin mine showing pump and sluice boxes

A tin dredge

Picking cotton (see page 94)

continually moves along. Tin dredges were first introduced just before the war. After the war they were installed in great numbers, and their efficiency has been very rapidly and greatly improved. In 1929 about 40 per cent. of the Malayan output was raised by dredges. Thus there is a variety of methods of mining in Malaya, and the same is true of the Dutch East Indies, where the Government virtually own and operate the whole industry. In Bolivia, however, ordinary underground mines have to be sunk to reach the ore; hence tin mining in Bolivia has always been a large-scale capitalist industry, and is now dominated by one big combine. The small Chinese partnerships and relatively small European companies of Malaya are virtually impossible in Bolivia.

The washing in sluice boxes leaves a mixture of which about 70 per cent. is tin. This mixture is then smelted. A large part of the Dutch East Indies output is normally smelted there or in Holland. The rest of the South-east Asia output is smelted in two big works, one at Singapore and the other at Penang. The Bolivian output and the Nigerian output cannot be smelted in those countries because there is no coal, and have always been smelted in Great Britain, largely because until recently the Bolivian ore could not be smelted easily unless it was mixed with other ores, and when in 1902 some Americans tried to set up a smelting plant in the United States, the British Government imposed a heavy tax on all ore from British colonies not being shipped to British smelters. For this and other reasons, the Americans have never been able to establish a smelting industry, although they are such big consumers of tin. A small amount of tin smelting is done in China, Australia and in Europe, but two British companies, one of which owns all the works in Great Britain and the works at Penang, and the other the works at Singapore, between them smelt 75 per cent. of the world's output. Great Britain has thus a commanding, and to some extent a monopolistic, position in the smelting of tin, quite apart from the Empire's position as a producer of 45 per cent. of the world's output.

To understand the recent story of tin and tin restriction, it is necessary once more to go back as far as the war. During the war and the post-war boom, tin went to a very high price, but this was primarily because of the difficulty of getting sufficient shipping to bring the tin from the far-away producing countries to Europe. Very large stocks accumulated in the East awaiting shipment, and when the post-war slump began in 1920, this accumulation of stocks, combined with the much reduced consumption, caused a collapse in the price. It seemed that something must be done to hold these stocks off the market, and so the British and Dutch Governments combined together to buy up some 17,000 tons, and to withhold it from the market until consumption revived and the price had reached a more normal level. Looking back in the light of subsequent events, one now realises that the holding-back, and subsequent gradual release, of these stocks blinded the market to the fact that consumption was running steadily more and more ahead of production during 1924 and 1925. If these stocks had not been added to the current new production, the price of tin would have risen much more rapidly and to a much higher level in 1924 and 1925, and this would have given a much clearer signal that additional productive capacity was required. As it was, the world did not fully appreciate the growing excess of consumption over production in time to arrange for increased capacity, and during 1926 there was a rapid rise in the price to a peak of over £300 per ton in February 1927. The world now awoke with a start to the realisation that considerable new capacity ought to be established as quickly as possible, but with this sudden awakening the amount required was greatly exaggerated. There was, of course, a boom in tin shares, and the flotation of a very large number of new companies, while existing companies increased their capacity. The mines in Bolivia also extended their capacity, though to a smaller extent.

In anticipation of increased supplies, the price of tin began to decline quite rapidly during 1927, but the big increase in production did not come until 1928, and still more in 1929. By the middle of 1929, it was clear that there would shortly be very considerable over-production even if consumption continued to increase. The appearance of the world trade depression at the beginning of 1930, and the consequent rapid decline in the demand for tin, turned what was already a serious position into a crisis of the first order.

It was the serious nature of the outlook for the near

future which led in July 1929 to the formation of the
Tin Producers' Association. At first comprising some
20 per cent. of the industry, the Association began even
at that time to advocate the need for restriction as a
remedy for the inevitable over-production. By November 1929, it was able to point out the increasingly
serious nature of the problem, and its membership
rapidly increased. In January 1930 the Association
advocated the stopping of all mining operations for
32 hours each week or its equivalent; but this proved
ineffective. In May, a voluntary curtailment of output
by 20 per cent. was agreed upon by the members of
the Association, both in Malaya and Nigeria, while the
output of a large proportion of the Bolivian mines was
similarly curtailed. Efforts were made to persuade the
Dutch to join the scheme, but their point of view was,
briefly, that they had not expanded production during
the boom to any appreciable extent, and that, therefore,
is was unreasonable to expect them to curtail operations
during the slump for the benefit of those countries who
had increased their production to an unwise extent.
This second effort at partial voluntary restriction was
not much more successful than the first. With the continuing contraction in consumption, the price had been
down as low as £105 by the end of 1930, and there was
probably a surplus of at least 20,000 tons of stocks over
and above the normal amount. The situation was
indeed desperate for the relatively high-cost producers,
such as Bolivia and Nigeria, while the majority of both
European and Chinese producers in Malaya could at

that time barely cover their costs; the same was broadly true of the Dutch industry.

In these critical circumstances the governments of the countries concerned were induced to intervene. Voluntary restriction had proved totally inadequate. The only hope was for a government compulsory scheme. Eventually the Dutch Government was induced to believe that its interests also lay in restriction, and in February 1931 the present international scheme was established for a period of six years, i.e. until December 31st, 1936. It may be observed in passing that the negotiations were conducted by the British Government from London, and not by the Government of Malaya, and that there was a very active opposition to the idea of restriction among some important groups of producers in Malaya, who argued that, as low-cost producers, they ought not to be penalised for the benefit of their high-cost competitors. As from January 1st, 1931, production was to be restricted to 78 per cent. of the 1929 output of each country. But the degree of restriction was successively and rapidly increased, because the price obstinately refused to rise, and equally stocks refused to fall. In August 1931, however, the special problem of the surplus stocks was attacked by the formation of a private pool which quickly purchased some 21,000 tons. These stocks were to be released in accordance with a sliding scale of quantities and prices, beginning at a price of £165 sterling. By July 1932 production was restricted to one-third of the 1929 output. This was definitely below even the much reduced consumption, and consumption very soon began to increase with the revival of trade in the United States. By May 1933 the price had risen to £180, and stocks had been reduced by 10,000 tons at least, while the machinery of the scheme had gradually been brought to a point where little or no leakage of supplies was taking place. During the autumn of 1933, as the result of this drastic restriction to one-third of capacity, and with the improvement in world trade generally, the price rapidly rose to a level of nearly £230 per ton, where it has, broadly speaking, remained. For the first quarter of 1934, output was allowed to increase from 33 to 40 per cent., and during the summer to 50 per cent. But consumption then showed signs of falling off, and restriction was tightened again in the autumn to 40 per cent. In 1934 also, the International Tin Committee agreed to buy tin on its own account in order to stop any undue fall in the price, and to sell tin if the price rose unduly. The declared object of this so-called buffer-pool scheme was to help to keep the price stable, but it has been much criticised as giving undesirable powers to the Committee over the tin market, powers which might easily be abused, and which some say have been abused during 1935. Yet another development in 1934 was that a number of the smaller producing countries were brought into the scheme. Naturally with the establishment of such high prices, producers outside the scheme increased their output, and the percentage of their output to the total world production rose from 10 per cent. in the years 1929–31 to 20 per cent. in 1933. From the point of view of the restricting countries it was essential that this should be stopped, but they had to offer very good terms to induce French Indo-China, the Belgian Congo, Portugal and Cornwall to join the scheme. However, their inclusion has made the scheme more complete, even if the cost is falling mostly on the original members.

During the spring of 1935 it appeared that it had been necessary for another private pool, as well as the official buffer pool, to purchase stocks in order to maintain the price, but little is known of the activities of this private pool, except that the International Tin Restriction Committee is said to have been privy to its operations. Despite the temporary break in the price of tin during the "pepper crisis" in March, the earlier decision to increase production quotas to 45 per cent. was maintained, and in July a further increase to 50 per cent. was allowed. But this quickly proved inadequate, and during the third quarter there was an increasing shortage of supplies, which was reflected in a big premium on tin for immediate delivery as compared with the price for future delivery. In August production quotas were increased from 50 to 65 per cent., retrospectively to July 1st. This will ease the shortage in due course, but the price for future delivery still ranges between £220 and £230, and for immediate delivery there is still a substantial premium.

At the moment therefore there is no gainsaying the fact that the scheme has achieved its objects—the surplus stocks have disappeared, and the price has been stabilised at a level which enables nearly all producers to make substantial profits even if their output is restricted to 40 per cent. When tin producers consider the position of most other raw material producers to-day, they must feel very satisfied that they embraced the gospel of restriction. And when one tries to imagine what would have happened if there had been no restriction scheme, the blessings of that scheme appear greater than ever. If there had been no restriction scheme, one might well have seen the price of tin fall as low as £50 per ton. At such a price-level, it is extremely questionable whether Bolivia could have continued to produce at all, and much the same would probably be true of Nigeria. A large percentage of the industry in Malaya would also have had to close down, while the financial difficulties of the Dutch East Indies Government would have been rendered still more acute than they actually have been. In short, the whole industry would have been completely disorganised, the owners of capital invested in tin mining would have suffered ruinous losses, while the economic life of a large part of at least two countries would have been virtually destroyed, and serious difficulties would have occurred in others. Restriction has, of course, meant very considerable unemployment amongst the mine workers, but no restriction might have been worse even from their point of view. And when the world depression really lifts, there might well be a shortage of tin supplies, another boom in price, and the need to replace a large part of the capacity which had been destroyed during the depression. Admittedly the present price of tin is high, but the consumer should regard this as an insurance against the possibility of still higher prices later on. And anyway, he seems quite willing to pay the present price.

That is, I hope, a fair statement of the case *for* the present restriction scheme, and the policy which is being pursued. As to its validity, different views will be held according as to whether the judge is a high-cost producer, a low-cost producer, or a consumer of tin. High-cost producers will have no hesitation in supporting the scheme, for otherwise they would probably by now be ruined. And they will clearly support the renewal of the present agreement when it expires at the end of 1936, and the continuation of the present policy for an indefinite period, since while it lasts they are making at least some profits, and if it stops they will soon be bankrupt. For even if the consumption of tin in due course increases so as to require the full operation of all the existing capacity, new capacity can and will be introduced with costs far below their costs, and that new capacity will take their place. High-cost producers, therefore, have everything to gain by restriction.

On the other hand, a new low-cost producer will take rather different views. Fundamentally he will want to be free to compete successfully with the high-cost producers, and drive them out of existence. Three years ago he may have felt that the middle of the worst trade depression ever experienced was not a very suitable time to carry this competition to extremes, and so he was not altogether displeased when his government set up the present restriction scheme. But now that world trade shows signs of some recovery, he begins to wonder whether restriction is really desirable, for he realises that though he may be benefiting, his high-cost competitors are benefiting still more, and in a way at his expense. Also he will be wondering whether the maintenance of the present price can be good for consumption, and whether it is not stimulating the use and invention of substitutes, to his detriment in the future. He himself would be quite satisfied with a much lower price, and he is beginning to wonder whether it can be wise to exploit the consumer for the benefit of inefficient or over-capitalised producers, and whether it would not be better to end restriction, and get through the admittedly difficult business of eliminating the high-cost producers, which must be done before the tin industry can regain any real stability.

And finally, what of the consumer's point of view? Above everything, what the manufacturer wants is stability in the price of tin, and if he could get that, he would not mind paying a little more than the competitive price for his tin. But when the well-known chairman of one of the biggest tin-mining companies in Malaya assures him that the East could produce at a profit all the tin required by the world at £100 per ton, and he is paying £230, the manufacturer rather naturally considers that the price of stability is altogether too high, and that the tin restriction scheme is nothing more or less than a grasping monopoly. Even if this figure of £100 is really too low, even if it is raised by 50 per cent., the present price seems from the consumer's point of view really outrageous. Naturally manufacturers are endeavouring to economise their use of tin and to develop substitutes, and in these days of scientific invention he would be a bold man who would deny the possibility that considerable success may attend such efforts.

The differing views of high-cost and low-cost producers and of the consumer will, of course, be reflected in the attitude of the governments of countries who are in these positions, and it must be remembered that the present restriction scheme rests upon an agreement between the governments of the producing countries, and not between the producers themselves. And here there is a complication, for one of the parties to the agreement, namely the British Government, covers both low-cost producers, as in Malaya, and relatively high-cost producers, as in Nigeria. With its predominance as a producer, with its commanding position as a smelter, and at the same time with Great Britain itself as a large consumer of tin, much depends upon the attitude of the British Government. Up to the present, the International Tin Restriction Scheme has been a great success, and may well be judged a sound and justifiable means of meeting the drastic fall in the demand for tin during the worst years of a very serious world trade depression. But the scheme has done little or nothing towards curing the underlying trouble of capacity in excess of requirements even under conditions of ordinary normal world trade activity. This excess of capacity must be cured before a true equilibrium can be re-established on the basis of a normal demand, and the longer restriction is maintained in its present form, so long will the trouble of excess capacity remain. Restriction may have been justifiable up to the present, and may even be so for a further short period, but there is bound to come a time, if it has not in fact already come, when further postponement of the competitive struggle between high-cost and low-cost producers, and therefore of the elimination of the excess capacity, will not be in the true interests of the industry as a whole and its future prosperity.

Postscript, December 10th, 1935. The shortage of supplies, described on p. 163 above, has continued during the last three months, though the situation is now easier since, at the beginning of October, production quotas were increased to 70 per cent. retrospectively to July 1st, and later to 80 per cent. retrospectively to October 1st, while it has just been announced that for the first quarter of 1936 the percentage will be 90. This 90 per cent. means an output of about 185,000 tons per annum, while consumption is not higher than 150,000 tons. It now seems clear that the International Committee is content with a price-level of £230, and is willing to release production as long as that level is maintained; the delay in doing so was apparently only an error of judgment, though one for which the consumer is having to pay somewhat dearly. A tremendous excess of supplies has thus been followed by an artificial shortage, and equilibrium of any kind has not yet been achieved.

Chapter VIII

THE TROUBLES WHICH GIVE RISE TO
RESTRICTION SCHEMES

WE have now examined the recent history of six of the more important foodstuffs and raw materials: what are the general impressions which these stories leave upon the mind? The first, and perhaps the most obvious, is that these industries are all in serious trouble of one kind or another: either the price of the product is unprofitable for a large proportion of the producers, because vast unwanted stocks have accumulated or because there is far too much producing capacity, or else the price would be unprofitable if resort had not been had to some form of artificial control. But a general world trade depression inevitably reduces the demand for almost everything below what it was before the depression began, and usually below the average demand of say the four or five years preceding the depression. Given a world trade depression, one would of course expect to find almost all industries in a depressed condition and facing very considerable difficulties. But most of us are probably aware that in this depression as compared with previous trade depressions, primary producers, that is producers of foodstuffs and raw materials as a group, have been exceptionally hard hit: the fall in the prices of primary products has exceeded all known records, and the difficulties of the great primary producing countries, though essentially the same as those experienced in previous world depressions, are unprecedented in their complex severity. Again, as the result of our historical studies, we know that most of our six industries were in trouble before the world depression began: this was definitely so in sugar, rubber and cotton, while in the case of tin, coffee and wheat serious trouble was clearly in prospect by 1929, and would certainly have overtaken these industries even if there had been no world depression. It seems clear in fact that if all the primary industries had been in a thoroughly healthy state of normal equilibrium before the depression began, the effects of the depression would have been much less severe than they actually have been: the special severity during this depression was due to the unhealthy state of these industries at the time when the depression commenced, just as the catching of a chill has usually more effect on a man who is already suffering from other complaints than on one in perfect health. If then we concentrate our attention in the first place on what was wrong in the years leading up to 1929, we ought to get a better explanation of the nature of the troubles from which the world's primary producers have been, and still are, suffering, than if we confine our attention simply to the last few years.

The equilibrium of an industry may be disturbed by changes affecting the demand for the product, or by changes affecting the supply, or by changes in both demand and supply. Let us take the demand side first. Did the demand for foodstuffs and raw materials as a whole fail to fulfil expectations? Did it either fail to increase as much as might reasonably be expected, or did it actually fall instead of increasing? According to the estimates of the Economic Section of the League of Nations, the consumption of foodstuffs was increasing slightly faster than the increase of population from 1925 to 1929, and the same would be true of the period 1913–29. The consumption of raw materials however increased by about 20 per cent. between 1925 and 1929, as compared with an increase of about 5 per cent. in population. These figures may not be very precise, but there is no denying two facts: (1) that the world was rapidly growing richer; (2) that the world was spending its increasing wealth not primarily on more foodstuffs but on more raw materials, that is on more manufactures or more capital equipment.

It is perhaps surprising that the consumption of foodstuffs per head has not increased more, but one would not expect it to increase very much, because the increase in incomes has been most marked in the Western Hemisphere, where most, though not all, people have enough food, and as they get richer, the tendency is to eat better food rather than more. But it is fairly certain that there has been no fall in food consumption, and though of course the consumption of certain foodstuffs, like wheat, has not expanded as fast as that of others, like sugar, we cannot say that there was up to 1929 any general failure of the demand, such as would greatly disturb the equilibrium of the food-producing industries; while in the case of raw materials, the expansion of demand certainly exceeded all expectations. Actually of our six commodities, the increase of the consumption of coffee was quite normal, that of sugar extremely large, though admittedly increasing less rapidly than in pre-war times, while the consumption of rubber and tin was increasing by leaps and bounds; in wheat and cotton the increase was less marked but still considerable, and one does not expect the demand for everything to expand uniformly. Speaking generally, therefore, I think it can be safely concluded that there was nothing fundamentally wrong on the demand side.

Let us then turn to the supply side. Since there was not much wrong with the demand, how is it that in so many industries conditions of excess capacity had arisen? The Great War can certainly be blamed to a considerable extent in some cases. The early troubles in sugar were very largely due to the mistaken view of Cuban and other producers that it would be a good many years before the beet-sugar industry of Europe recovered to anything approaching its pre-war output. The accumulation of stocks of tin in the East as the result of the shipping shortage, and of the post-war slump, led to the government stock-holding scheme which, as I have argued, delayed the introduction of the increased capacity which was required, and so was in part responsible for the exceptional boom of 1926–27 which led to the introduction of too much new capacity.

Most important of all, perhaps, was the effect of the war in destroying the great wheat exports of Russia and the Danubian countries, and so causing the expansion of wheat production in countries like Canada. But the war cannot be made directly or chiefly responsible for all the trouble in these industries, nor for any large part of the trouble in other industries. It does not play much part in the stories of coffee or cotton, and though the post-war slump gave rise to the British Rubber Restriction Scheme, it was purely the handling of that scheme which led to the creation of so much new capacity. The troubles of coffee also were caused by the mistakes made in administering the control scheme. On the other hand, in cotton the trouble was due primarily to the development of new areas of supply, and to the rising costs of production in the American cotton belt. In short, the causes of the trouble appear to be, in the main, different in each industry, and it is not easy to see any general common cause.

Nevertheless the very generality of trouble in so many primary industries makes a very strong *prima-facie* case in favour of a common source. Let us cast round for a new trail. What other impressions have been left on our minds by the previous chapters? I think one must be the rapidity of technical progress in the widest sense of that term. I have described the opening-up on a vast scale of new coffee lands in Brazil, new sugar lands in Cuba, and the introduction of a new variety of cane in Java with a 30 per cent. greater yield of sugar, the development of rubber forests in the Dutch East Indies whose native owners are prepared to produce rubber very cheaply, and the reduction in the costs of production by European estates; the introduction of the tin dredge, and its rapid improvement so that ground which was worked over a few years ago can now be profitably re-worked at a very much lower price than that which rules to-day; the development of new low-cost cotton areas, and the revolutionising by machinery of wheat production in the great exporting countries. Technical progress in this wide sense has obviously been very rapid during the last few years, but to a large extent it has taken forms of which the older producers cannot take advantage. We have seen how true this is of wheat production in Europe; and where technical progress takes the form, not primarily of new and better machinery, but of new and richer sources of supply, there is bound to be excess capacity until the old high-cost producers have been forced to abandon production. An economic system in which technical progress is very rapid, must possess great elasticity and adaptability among its various parts; labour must be mobile, in a geographical sense and as between one industry and another, while capital must be both enterprising and venturesome, or the whole machine may cease to operate smoothly and effectively.

Now, particularly in the case of foodstuffs, there is another and wider aspect. If, as the world grows richer, it wants very little more staple foodstuffs per head of the population, and if the progress of technique enables a given output to be obtained with constantly less and less labour, then it follows that proportionately less and less of the world's population will be required to produce foodstuffs. Fundamentally the position is that a smaller and smaller proportion of each year's new labour supplies is required to produce foodstuffs, if indeed it is not a case of having to reduce the present amount of labour so engaged. Fundamentally the need is to divert more and more men away from the land and into manufacturing industry and other services. If this does not happen on the required scale, we should expect to find wages and incomes in agriculture lagging behind wages and incomes in manufacturing industry, and this is precisely what we do find to be the case during the last ten or fifteen years. Taking the world as a whole, real wages in agriculture from 1924 to 1929 were stationary, if not tending to decline, while real wages in manufacturing industry were rising fast. Much the same was really true of the production of raw materials, though, owing to the expansion in manufacturing output, the demand for most raw materials was rapidly increasing, and so the necessary adjustment was smaller. Therefore, if maximum production at minimum cost was to be secured, and if the whole economic system was to work reasonably smoothly, the rapid technical progress of the last fifteen to twenty years demanded very rapid adjustments in the distribution of capital and labour as between different occupations, and therefore in many cases as between different countries. But here we reach another serious and fairly general source of trouble, namely the growth of economic nationalism.

Economic nationalism is sometimes positive, that is when the production of some commodity is subsidised and protected in order to safeguard the nation's supplies of that commodity in the event of war, or in order to maintain a peasant community for military or social reasons, or possibly in order to prevent mono-polistic extortion by a combination of producers in other countries. Sugar and wheat provide some good examples of this kind of economic nationalism. But economic nationalism is also a negative and defensive policy, and that is the kind which has been most important so far as the primary industries are con-cerned during recent years, and still is so to-day. Existing national industries, which were threatened by lower-cost producers in other countries, and which ought to have disappeared in whole or in part, have been defended and protected by higher and higher tariffs and bounties, because their disappearance would involve much loss of capital, substantial unemployment for a time, and all the general financial, political and social difficulties which are involved in any large-scale redistribution of national resources. This kind of government intervention was fairly widespread even before 1929, and was an important factor in creating the trouble which in turn gave rise to artificial control schemes. But at the end of 1929 the whole situation was changed by the onset of the world depression. No longer was the world's demand for foodstuffs or even

raw materials expanding; on the contrary every industry found the demand for its products declining
day by day in a manner which suggested that the
process would only stop at zero. Those industries which
were already top-heavy with excess capacity as the
result of the natural lack of elasticity and adaptability
in our economic system, and of the artificial hindrances
which governments and high-cost producers had been
putting in the way of the necessary readjustments,
soon found themselves in a sinking condition. Producers appealed to their governments for aid, and
governments could not turn a deaf ear, for the whole
economic, political, and social structure of their countries seemed threatened with collapse. The defensive
measures of the years of general world prosperity were
naturally increased when the world depression rendered
already serious situations absolutely critical, and
governments the world over have done everything
they could think of to reduce the impact of the storm
on their particular countries. In many industries, the
high-cost producers were in old-established economically
powerful countries, which were thus able to afford the
heavy expense of fairly effective protection, with the
result that the low-cost producers have borne the full
brunt of the decreased demand. Consequently the
extent of the adjustments which are now required if
the world's economic system is to give maximum production at minimum cost, or even to work in any
reasonable and common-sense way, is greater than
ever.

It is against such a general background that we have to study the merits and demerits of schemes for the artificial control of primary products. We have to study in detail the uses to which such schemes have been put, both in the period of general world prosperity, and in the subsequent period of general world depression; and we have to assess the good and evil of the results so far achieved. We have to try and analyse the conditions which must be observed if valorisation schemes, such as the Brazilian coffee scheme, are not to end in such disastrous results as has been the case. We have to try and analyse the conditions under which restriction schemes will be more advantageous than a policy of *laissez-faire*, and the conditions under which they will be less advantageous. These are no easy tasks, and I must warn the reader that the chapters which follow are not as easy reading as I hope he will have experienced hitherto. But understanding and knowledge are never to be had without effort, and understanding and knowledge as to the proper uses of this new invention in economic organisation may at least save us from costly repetitions of past mistakes, and perhaps from some new ones.

Chapter IX

THE ECONOMICS OF RESTRICTION SCHEMES
IN WORLD PROSPERITY

HAVING studied the recent history of a number of the more important attempts at artificial control of the supplies of foodstuffs and raw materials, we are now in a position to consider in general the whole issue of artificial or conscious control versus the unconscious control of the competitive *laissez-faire* system under modern conditions; and, as was said at the end of the previous chapter, we have to pass judgment on all these new methods of industrial organisation with a view to our guidance in the future. It is clear however that the kind of control which was aimed at by the Brazilian coffee growers, the Wheat Pools, and at the start by the Federal Farm Board in respect of American cotton, was fundamentally different from that of the control schemes for sugar, rubber and tin. The former aimed at equalising or regularising the supply offered for sale, despite the variations from year to year in the actual crops: the latter sought to reduce the actual volume of production. The former were valorisation schemes, using that word in its more strictly interpreted sense of valorisation of producers' incomes, but not of the long-run average price of their product: the latter were restriction schemes. It will be simpler to consider these two main kinds of control schemes separately, and as restriction schemes are much more numerous, and in a sense more important, we will consider them first, and postpone a study of the economics of valorisation schemes until the last chapter.

Confining ourselves then to control schemes involving the principle of restriction of output, we may for convenience of study make a further classification. The Wall Street crash of October 1929 ended a longish period of general prosperity, and ushered in the general world trade depression from which the world is still only very slowly recovering. Thus the restriction schemes which were in existence before the Wall Street crash had been established, and were operating, in conditions of general world prosperity, whereas, since October 1929, restriction schemes have been operating in conditions of general world depression and distress. Of course the industries concerned in the pre-1929 schemes were not prosperous—restriction schemes would never have been established if they had been—but these industries were exceptional, whereas since 1929 all industries have been depressed, though in varying degree. Obviously a policy of restriction of output under conditions of general prosperity is a very different thing to restriction under conditions of general depression, and we will therefore consider first the period of prosperity ending in October 1929—that is the pre-1929 restriction schemes.

Among the industries which we have studied there were two important pre-1929 restriction schemes—

those in rubber and sugar—but we may also pay a little
attention to restriction in the copper industry, and the
discussions concerning the need for restriction in the
tin industry which were initiated in the summer of 1929.
The first thing which must strike the reader of the
chapters on rubber and sugar, is the different nature of
the troubles for which restriction was applied as the
appropriate remedy. Let us consider these schemes
in turn.

The main trouble in the rubber industry, which led
to the British rubber restriction scheme of 1922, was
the temporary decline in the anticipated or normal
growth of the demand for rubber, owing to the post-
war depression and its special severity in the United
States during 1921. It is true that the existing capacity
for production was somewhat in excess of the demand
which might reasonably have been expected if there
had been no post-war depression, and that the increase
in capacity, which was daily occurring as newly planted
trees reached tappable size, was somewhat greater than
the anticipated increase in the demand; but this excess
of capacity was not a very serious matter, especially
as, in general, costs of production on the older plantations were not appreciably higher than costs on the
new plantations, and so there was no problem of
surplus obsolete capacity: at the worst the demand
would catch up to the supply within a comparatively
short time, or at least this was the outlook based on
the knowledge as to the scale of recent new plantings
which was then possessed by the leaders of the industry.

Thus the essential trouble seemed to be the decline in the demand, which would presumably be only temporary, and it seemed perfectly sound to introduce a restriction scheme to tide the industry over the interval; otherwise cut-throat competition would ensue, and might well result in the bankruptcy, and even the disappearance, of a substantial amount of capacity which was neither inefficient nor obsolete, and which would probably be required again in the near future. This seems a reasonably sound line of argument, and we may provisionally accept it as such. It is true that the scheme did not include all the producers—the refusal of the Dutch to co-operate was a serious weakness, as the Stevenson Committee fully realised. But if we assume that the Committee expected the necessity for the scheme to end within, say, two or three years, its final decision to proceed without the Dutch was reasonable, bearing in mind that newly planted trees would not be in production until more than twice that length of time; the Dutch would gain at the expense of British producers, but no permanent harm would result, and there would still be a net advantage to British producers as compared with *laissez-faire*. The British rubber restriction scheme was initially a sound enough proposition from the economic point of view. It failed, not because it was fundamentally unsound, but because it was not removed when the demand recovered, and, instead, was converted into an attempt at monopolistic exploitation of the consumer. Consumers retaliated, and, as time went on, the degree of monopolistic power became considerably smaller, for the plantings of the war and immediate post-war years, especially by the natives in the Dutch East Indies, were found to be much greater than had been supposed; while during the high-price period of 1925–27, these same Dutch natives, and various other "outside" producers, were planting on a scale so prodigious that the monopolistic power of producers in British territories would clearly be completely lost in the future, unless the scheme was abandoned and the price allowed to fall: moreover the new planting already threatened to result in a future total capacity far in excess of the estimated future demand. All the disastrous history of the latter years of the scheme does not however undermine the validity of the proposition that the scheme as originally established was sound, and that if it had been brought to an end when the demand recovered, say in 1924 or early 1925, all would probably have been well, and the loss to producers and their countries as the result of the post-war depression would have been considerably less than it would have been under *laissez-faire.*

Turning now to the Cuban sugar industry, we find a very different set of conditions. The fundamental trouble here was the unexpectedly rapid recovery of the European beet-sugar industry after its war-time devastation, and, in general, the expansion of subsidised or protected supplies in consuming countries, notably in the United States and its overseas possessions, and in the British Empire. There was nothing

much wrong with the growth of the world's demand
for sugar as a whole, even though it was less rapid per
head than in the pre-war period; the trouble was that
the increase of world supplies was greater. The situation
was made worse because a considerable expansion of
capacity had been undertaken in Cuba itself during
the previous eighteen months or two years, on the
assumption that it would be several years before the
European beet-sugar industry regained its pre-war output. This was a great and costly mistake; but even if there
had been no such expansion, Cuba would still have had
to face the problem of a decline in the demand for her
sugar due to the determination of her chief customers
to produce themselves the whole, or at least a substantial part, of their requirements. Of course at the
end of 1925 the Cuban producers were hoping that the
effect of the subsidies and protection in Europe and the
United States had more or less run its course, and that
therefore if they could weather another season or two
the normal growth in demand would catch up with the
increased supply, and that the enlarged Cuban crop
would then be required. But even on these assumptions, the case for a general restriction scheme was
very weak, because a substantial proportion of the
Cuban capacity had become relatively high-cost and
obsolescent. Many of the Cuban-owned mills in the
western half of the island were old, small, and inefficiently equipped, while they drew their supplies of
cane from land which was becoming exhausted after
twenty-five or more years of continuous cropping. The

expansions of the war years, and of 1923–25, had brought into existence large modern mills in the eastern half of the island, equipped and operated by American engineers and scientists, and drawing their cane from virgin land which had been laid out to facilitate the utmost use of mechanical tillage and transport. In consequence, the costs of these new mills were little more than half those of the old mills, and despite the great expansion which had occurred, there was still plenty of virgin land available for yet more new mills. Sooner or later new low-cost mills were going to take the place of the old high-cost mills. If the Cuban hopes of 1925 had actually been realised, if, that is, the demand for Cuban sugar had recovered and resumed a reasonable rate of growth, the price would have risen, but before it had reached a level profitable to the highest-cost producers, it would have paid to establish further new mills, which would have therefore replaced them. Actually the Cuban hopes of 1925 were not to be realised—the effect of the tariffs and bounties encouraging home production by Cuba's chief customers was not nearly spent—and therefore Cuba was in fact faced with a demand which was gradually shrinking to still lower levels, and would not recover unless and until consuming countries radically changed their policies in respect of home-produced sugar supplies.

Under such conditions restriction is obviously no remedy: the object of a restriction scheme is to preserve the capacity of an industry intact, whereas with a permanent fall in the demand, there must clearly be a reduction of capacity. The old high-cost mills had got to face destruction sooner or later, and in 1926 the world in general was enjoying a period of relative and increasing prosperity, and this was specially true of Cuba's nearest and greatest potential general market, the United States, while general economic conditions in the Cuban home market were relatively favourable. In 1926, the inevitable diversion of Cuban labour and capital from the production of sugar to the production of other more marketable products would have been extremely difficult, as all such large-scale and sudden diversions are. But every year of delay was to be a year nearer to a serious and prolonged world depression, the incidence of which was to be specially acute in the United States; and restriction merely meant delay. Cuba had to swallow a particularly nasty dose of the medicine of economic readjustment sooner or later: there was nothing which could be gained by delay, and, as it turned out, there was much to lose. It is easy to be wise after the event, but, at the time, the case for restriction was distinctly weak even on the assumption of a relatively short-period decline in the demand for Cuban sugar, while on the assumption of a permanent decline, the case against restriction was overwhelming. From the Cuban restriction scheme, we may therefore draw the conclusions, first, that restriction is no remedy for a permanent decline in demand; and, secondly, that restriction is likely to be an unsound policy, even as a means of meeting a temporary decline in demand, if any substantial proportion of the productive capacity of the industry is so high-cost that it will pay to introduce new capacity to take its place; if in addition the capacity is excessive, the case against restriction is of course all the stronger. For convenience I may here repeat the conclusion which we drew from the British rubber restriction scheme, namely that restriction is an appropriate means of meeting a temporary decline in demand where no such complications are present, that is where the capacity is in general efficient, and not in excess of what seems likely to be required when the demand recovers.

Our studies of particular commodities have not included copper, but, without going into too lengthy detail, let us see whether from the copper control scheme we can confirm these conclusions or add new ones. The trouble in the American copper industry, which led in 1926 to the establishment of the world marketing organisation known as Copper Exporters Inc., under which restriction of output was organised, was an excess of capacity beyond the requirements of the demand if the price was to be profitable to the higher-cost producers. The demand during the Great War had been virtually insatiable, and the output of copper had been greatly expanded, especially in the United States. The war peak was reached in 1916–17, and the peace-time demand did not reach that level until 1927. That the industry should suffer from excess capacity during the intervening ten years is therefore understandable, but if this was all the story, it would seem strange that the industry should have adopted a restriction scheme just at the moment when equilibrium between demand and supply was at last within sight. The rest of the story however puts the whole matter in a different light. A good deal of the expansion of capacity during the war years took the form of opening new mines and new seams which could only be worked profitably at the very high war-time price-level, or the reopening of old sources of supply to which the same condition applied. But during the immediate post-war years, new deposits were exploited, especially in Chile and Peru, for, with the aid of a rapidly advancing technique, they could be profitably worked even at the relatively low level to which the price had fallen owing to the fact that the capacity of the industry was already excessive. Thus, despite conditions of excess capacity, still further new capacity was created, and although in 1926 the demand was at last regaining its war-time peak and showed every sign of further rapid expansion, there seemed little probability of any substantial rise in price, and therefore of the higher-cost mines being able to operate profitably. They had not done so for years, and by 1926 the strain had become intolerable.

Now the American copper industry was comparatively highly organised, and ownership was closely concentrated, so that to a large extent the big companies were owners of both high-cost and low-cost mines within the United States, while some of them also owned new low-cost mines in Chile and Peru. If this had not been the case, many of the high-cost mines

would probably have been forced into bankruptcy
before 1926, and the new low-cost mines would, so to
speak, have taken their place, whereas in fact they
simply added to the already excessive capacity; the big
companies carried them on, for they were unwilling to
write off their book values. In short, the position was
that to a considerable extent the low-cost properties
were carrying the high-cost on their backs. Again,
owing to this common ownership, a restriction scheme
was a possibility, for otherwise the low-cost concerns
would obviously never have agreed to it. Restriction
was introduced in order to keep the high-cost mines
alive for a little longer, and, if possible, to enable them
to yield a little more profit before their owners were
finally forced to close them down for good. Needless
to say, this was not the ground on which the restriction
scheme was justified publicly, and indeed few outside
observers were at the time fully able to realise the
true position. The restriction scheme was introduced
on the ground that it was desirable to eliminate short-
period fluctuations in the price, and the profits which
merchants and speculators made thereby. Frequent
and rapidly fluctuating prices for copper were alleged
to be a cause of serious loss and inconvenience to
manufacturers, and still more so to producers, whose
output rate must be determined many months before
the copper reaches the market: merchant-speculators
of all kinds were the source of this evil, and also the
only persons who benefited: incidentally the merchant-
speculators were mostly located outside the United

States, to wit in London. There was a good deal of truth in all this, but it must be realised that the excess of supplies inevitably meant a "buyers' market", and naturally in such circumstances sellers feel that their interests are not well served. But while the scheme was ostensibly designed to give producers greater control over the market and the price-level, its real object, as its subsequent history clearly shows, was to introduce restriction of output, and so to raise the price-level, in order to help the high-cost producers in the circumstances already described.

It is clear that under such conditions a restriction scheme was simply a deliberate attempt to exploit the consumer. If the scheme raised the price sufficiently to enable the high-cost obsolescent mines to make a profit, then the consumer would be paying for something which he did not want, namely the preservation of capacity which could only produce, in the long run, at a price above that which would be adequate to induce the establishment of new capacity to supply his needs. If the control were to maintain such a price-level for any length of time, it would obviously have to prevent the establishment of any new capacity. Copper Exporters Inc. was in fact unable to exert complete control over its members within the United States, still less in Chile and Peru even though many of these mines were owned by its members, still less again over its foreign associated members, particularly Katanga, and not at all over any new producers who might appear in any other part of the world, the most likely being in Rhodesia. Thus, even as an attempt at monopolistic exploitation, Copper Exporters Inc. was an extremely risky performance from the point of view of those concerned, as well as being quite unjustifiable from the consumer's point of view. Some of those concerned doubtless believed that the scheme would restore equilibrium to the industry, that, in short, it was a remedy for the troubles arising from excessive capacity. They argued that before long the demand would increase sufficiently to require the whole existing capacity, and that to preserve the whole existing capacity, so to speak, in cold storage, was therefore the only sensible course. But they were either ignorant of the facts, or they blindly overlooked the obvious corollary, that unless the scheme was to be permanent, further new capacity would be established to take the place of the existing high-cost capacity, because that new capacity with its low costs would be able to make good profits at a price which would be ruinous to the existing high-cost producers. Under such conditions, the obsolete high-cost capacity must be eliminated if equilibrium is to be restored, and the quicker the better. Restriction under such circumstances only postpones the operation, and with capacity increasing so fast in Katanga, and the probable development of a large new, cheap source of supply in Rhodesia, it was most advisable for the American copper interests as a whole to put their house in order as quickly as possible. Restriction merely meant postponement, and there was nothing to be gained thereby even with the outlook as it appeared in 1926, while the future was in fact to show that everything was to be lost.

The reader will be aware that much the same as this was said about the Cuban sugar restriction scheme. Fundamentally the conditions were the same on the supply side, though totally different on the demand side. We can in fact modify and widen the conclusion which we drew from the Cuban restriction scheme, namely that restriction is likely to be an unsound policy as a means of meeting a temporary decline in demand, if the existing capacity of the industry is excessive, and a substantial proportion of it so high-cost that new capacity will be established at a price-level below that at which the high-cost capacity can earn profits. We can now say that restriction will be an equally unsound policy even if the demand is expanding in a normal way. The actual history of the copper control clearly supports this conclusion. Copper Exporters was for a time successful; restriction of output was at first more or less successfully established, though within the United States it had, of course, to be of a voluntary character owing to the Anti-Trust laws; control over the market was secured by the virtual elimination of the merchant-speculator; the price was raised considerably during 1928; and in the spring of 1929 consumers, scared by the apparent shortage of supplies, played into the hands of the control, and the price was eventually "stabilised" at a fantastically high level. This led not only to the refusal of many of the American producers to obey the call of Copper Exporters Inc. to resume the bonds of restriction, but it greatly stimulated the development of new capacity, especially the nascent industry in Rhodesia. At the same time the world depression began, and the demand declined severely during the winter of 1929–30. Copper Exporters held on to its price until April 1930, despite the piling up of enormous stocks, and then lost all control, leaving the whole industry, and particularly the American section, in the most parlous plight. But even if a much less greedy price policy had been pursued, and even if there had been no world depression to reduce the demand, the scheme was bound to fail in the end: there could be no return to equilibrium until the virtually obsolete capacity had been eliminated. Restriction could only serve the interests of the high-cost producers; from the point of view of the industry as a whole it was at best useless, and might well be harmful, as was the case; from the point of view of the consumer it was indefensible.

Finally let us just glance at the tin situation in 1929. Here as with copper, but unlike Cuban sugar, there was no fault to be found with the demand, which up to midsummer of that year had been increasing by leaps and bounds. But the great price boom of 1926–27 had brought into existence a very large amount of new capacity, most of which was much lower-cost than the existing capacity, simply because of the rapidity with which year by year the technique of production was being improved. The tin dredge of 1928–29 was a vastly more efficient machine than its predecessor of even a few years before. But not all the new capacity was low-cost: during the boom, production, especially in Bolivia and Nigeria, had been expanded by developing mines which could only pay at relatively high prices. As a result of the boom, the industry had, or would shortly have when all the new capacity had been completed, a total capacity far in excess of the requirements of the demand for several years to come, even assuming that the demand continued to expand; and the price of tin threatened to fall as low as it had recently been high. Again the argument was being raised for restriction as a method of cold storage until the demand caught up with the potential supply. And again we can reply that the preservation of high-cost capacity, when it pays to introduce low-cost capacity to take its place, is no possible remedy, and that restriction in such circumstances can only postpone the inevitable. Tin restriction in 1929 had only reached the discussion stage: but this glance at the situation does supply another example of a restriction scheme being applied in circumstances where, even if there had been no world depression, it would have been nothing but a hindrance.

Chapter X

THE ECONOMICS OF RESTRICTION SCHEMES
IN WORLD DEPRESSION

IN the previous chapter we have studied the economics of restriction schemes during the period of
general trade prosperity ending in 1929: we have now
to study the economics of restriction schemes under
conditions of general world depression since 1929. But
before we embark on this second half of our task, it
will perhaps be convenient to summarise the conclusions which we have already reached. These conclusions all relate to restriction schemes in times of
world prosperity, and may be set out shortly as follows:

(1) Restriction is *unsound* as a means of meeting a
permanent decline in demand, and is more than likely
to intensify the difficulties of the inevitable readjustment of resources.

(2) Restriction is *sound* as a means of meeting a
temporary decline in the demand provided that no
substantial proportion of the productive capacity is in
an advanced stage of obsolescence, this proviso being
of special importance if there was any tendency towards
excess capacity before the demand declined.

(3) Restriction is *unsound* as a remedy for troubles
arising from excess capacity, unless the productive
technique, in the widest sense of that term, is virtually stationary: it merely postpones the necessary

readjustments, and is therefore almost certain to make matters worse.

In respect of both the second and the third conclusions, we may perhaps further stress the point that much depends upon the current rate of the progress of productive technique in the industry concerned, and we may draw attention to the fact that during the nineteen-twenties productive technique was advancing with marked rapidity in nearly all the primary industries: it was certainly one of the direct causes of excess capacity in copper and tin, while it was a serious complication in sugar and rubber, and also in coffee and wheat.

It would perhaps be a logical procedure to draw conclusions concerning restriction in times of world depression from the history of restriction schemes since 1929, just as we have drawn the conclusions set out above for times of world prosperity. But there is one great objection and difficulty in so doing, namely that all the more important post-1929 schemes are still in operation, and so their history is not yet in any sense complete. Strictly speaking, this is also true of the pre-1929 schemes—their effects are by no means fully worked out, as for example those of the British rubber scheme—but the onset of the world depression so radically altered the whole situation that we may, with due caution, reasonably act as we have done, and consider the stories of these pre-1929 schemes sufficiently complete to warrant the deduction of provisional conclusions, provided that we exercise due care and discretion. But the stories of the post-1929 schemes are

by no means sufficiently complete for such purposes:
they have not in several important cases, such as
rubber or tin, even reached a stage where one can guess
the nature of the end with any reasonable certainty.
It seems therefore preferable to alter our method of
investigation, and instead of deducing the economics
of restriction schemes in depression from the recorded
history of such restriction schemes, let us try and
formulate conclusions by a process of abstract reasoning,
working from the conclusions we have already drawn
respecting restriction schemes in prosperity: then,
having formulated these abstract or *a priori* conclusions,
we shall of course try to see how far they are supported
or weakened by the incomplete historical evidence
which is available up to the time of writing. This
method of investigation has its drawbacks, of which
perhaps the chief is that having reached an abstract
conclusion, the investigator inevitably approaches his
subsequent study of the available facts with a certain
degree of bias, and is apt to misread the meaning of
the facts, however scientifically minded he tries to be.
But, despite its drawbacks, this method of investigation often yields results of considerable value at a stage
when the method of deduction fails to yield any results
at all, because the data are at present insufficiently
complete to show the investigator the key point in his
problem. We must, in practical life, work largely on
the basis of probabilities, and the justification for our
change of method is that it is better to foresee probabilities even of the "long-odds" type, than to foresee

nothing, which I think is what would follow from the exclusive use of the historical deductive method at the time of writing.

In the spring of 1930 most people realised that a period of relative prosperity had come to an end, and that the world's economic affairs were in process of violent dislocation. But most of us imagined that, at the worst, the world was being gripped by another of the general trade depressions of which so many had been experienced before; that, as in the past, this breath-taking grip would be relaxed in the course of a year or two; and that then recovery would be fairly rapid. We now know enough to say that fundamentally this depression is similar to previous world depressions, but that it has proved to be more severe and more lasting than any previously experienced, while recovery has been, and seems likely still to be, correspondingly slow. Essentially however the situation has been and still is that the primary industries, like all other industries, have been experiencing a severe fall in demand, but that in most, though not all, cases this fall in demand is of a temporary character, and that in due course the demand will recover to its 1929 level, and subsequently expand to a new and still higher peak. Let us for the moment exclude the exceptional cases where the demand may be permanently contracting, and confine ourselves to the problem of meeting a fall in the demand for the product of an industry, which, however severe, is nevertheless of a temporary character.

Now according to conclusion No. 2, set forth above on the basis of pre-1929 history, restriction should be a perfectly sound method of alleviating the situation, and one which has considerable potential advantages over *laissez-faire*, especially if the fall in the demand is severe, provided that no substantial proportion of the productive capacity is in an advanced stage of obsolescence, or, in other words, cannot operate profitably at a price below that which will induce the establishment of new capacity. For under *laissez-faire*, if the decline in demand is severe, the price will have to fall so low that current output is reduced to the smaller volume demanded, and producers who have not adequate financial reserves may be forced into bankruptcy, though they are as efficient, or even perhaps more efficient, than those who have such reserves. Even a forced cessation of production without full care and maintenance of the idle plant, will seriously impair the future efficiency of that plant, while bankruptcy may mean its virtual destruction, for in the conditions of the moment there may be no buyers of the bankrupt concern even at a knock-out price. A restriction scheme would enable the existing producers to weather the storm, and as the demand recovered, equilibrium would be regained, and restriction would automatically become unnecessary. From the consumer's point of view, though the price under restriction would be higher than under *laissez-faire* during the depression, it would be no higher in the long run, because under *laissez-faire* the total effective capacity of the industry might well be substantially reduced; and so, when the demand recovered, there would be a shortage of supplies, and the price would for a time rise abnormally high, pending the establishment of new capacity to take the place of the equally efficient capacity which had been destroyed. Thus the consumer would not be injured in the long run, and might well gain, for the industry would require less of his savings if perfectly efficient capital was not being unnecessarily destroyed. The gain from the producer's point of view in such a case is obvious, while, even if the decline in the demand was relatively small and short-lived, restriction would avoid much disorganisation and considerable financial difficulties, for which, even under *laissez-faire,* the consumer must pay in one form or another. Thus the case for restriction as a means of meeting a temporary decline in the demand seems thoroughly sound.

But we must not forget to pay proper respect to the proviso about the nature of the existing capacity in the industry. If a substantial proportion of the productive capacity is in an advanced stage of obsolescence, the cold storage process of a restriction scheme cannot rejuvenate it. On the contrary it will continue to grow more obsolete as every month and year passes, for there is little reason to suppose that technical progress stops during world trade depressions; indeed it usually quickens in hard times, though the general adoption of improvements is sometimes held up during the worst of a depression by difficulty in securing the requisite capital. Thus, where there is obsolescent capacity, the case for restriction as a means of meeting a temporary decline in demand is seriously weakened, and the longer recovery seems likely to be delayed, the stronger do the objections become. Sooner or later such obsolescent capacity must disappear, and from the point of view of the efficient producers in the industry there seems little point in delaying this disappearance, especially if restriction would otherwise be unnecessary, or its establishment postponed and its severity diminished; while from the point of view of the consumer there seems to be little or no point in paying for the maintenance of capacity which at the best will only be required for a very short time; it might well be better to risk an interval of relatively high prices before the requisite new capacity can be established. Therefore, if there is such obsolescent capacity, and if in addition the total capacity of the industry were in excess of the demand before the temporary decline in the demand occurred, the case against restriction would seem to become very strong indeed. It would seem that conclusion No. 8 then becomes applicable, namely that restriction is unsound as a remedy for troubles arising from excessive capacity unless productive technique is virtually stationary. If obsolescence on an appreciable scale is occurring, then productive technique cannot be stationary, and if there is excess capacity before the temporary fall in the demand occurs, then the troubles of the industry are partly due to excess capacity and partly to the decline in the demand. Restriction is a sound method of meeting the decline in the demand, but for curing excess capacity restriction is useless and only too likely to make matters worse. In short, when an industry, already top-heavy with excess and virtually obsolete capacity, encounters a serious decline in the demand for its products due to a world trade depression, it looks as if a restriction scheme should not be established until the low prices of *laissez-faire* have reduced the industry's capacity, at least to correspond with the demand before the world trade depression began, and probably rather below that. Then, if under *laissez-faire* the amputation of capacity seems likely to continue, or even if the efficiency of the remaining producers seems likely to be seriously impaired, a restriction scheme can be legitimately introduced, pending the passing of the depression.

Now if we apply these propositions to the primary industries when in 1930 they found themselves in the grip of the present world depression, we reach some rather disquieting conclusions. The restriction schemes which have been established or re-established since 1929, are nearly all in industries which were already suffering from excess capacity before the world depression began: this is obviously true of sugar, rubber, copper and tin, and also of Brazilian coffee, while it was on the verge of becoming true in the case of American cotton, and even of wheat. Of other products, which we have not studied in the preceding chapters, it is true of petroleum, and to some extent of

lead and zinc. On the whole it is not true of tea, for
which a restriction scheme has been established, and
it is certainly not true of wool, flax, jute, or meat
products, for which no proper restriction schemes have
been established, though a certain amount of local
government regulation has been enforced in some of
these industries. In short, those industries which were
already suffering from excess capacity, and therefore
ought not, according to our analysis, to have established
restriction schemes until that excess capacity had been
amputated, have in fact done so—for in none of these
industries had much capacity been destroyed before
the restriction scheme was brought into operation—
while most of those industries which might legitimately
have established restriction schemes, since their troubles
were solely due to the world trade depression, have not
done so. This is, to say the least of it, a little disquieting,
and may well prompt us to review our analysis.

Let us reconsider first the case for restriction as a
sound means of meeting a temporary decline in demand,
where the industry concerned is not suffering from
excess or obsolescent capacity. Look at it how one
may, there does not seem any flaw in our analysis of
this problem: artificial control here seems definitely
superior to *laissez-faire*, at least in theory. In practice,
however, one must not forget that this is essentially a
balance of disadvantages, not of advantages, from the
point of view of the producers. A restriction scheme
has its drawbacks—it always involves a great deal of
complicated administrative machinery; it often in-

volves the dislocation of speculative markets, and the antagonism of merchant-speculators and middlemen generally, whose services are most valuable in normal times; it demands faith in the integrity of those controlling the scheme as well as in their ability; and unless the scheme covers every producer, it will greatly benefit the outsiders temporarily, and even perhaps permanently. These drawbacks are in total considerable, and there is always the risk that they may prove far more serious than is anticipated. If then the anticipated disadvantages of *laissez-faire* appear only slightly greater than the anticipated disadvantages of restriction, the industry may well feel disinclined to make the grand-scale experiment which every restriction scheme involves. If the decline in the demand does not seem very great, or alternatively unlikely to last long, and especially if the industry is one in which producers can quickly adapt their productive organisation to a reduced scale of output without unduly increasing their costs, the industry may feel that under such conditions the evils and hardships of *laissez-faire*, of which they have had previous experience, are not so serious as to warrant experiments in artificial control, of which they have had no experience, and which undoubtedly seem risky and not too successful in other industries. Along some such grounds as these, it is probably correct to explain the non-appearance of a restriction scheme in the wool industry. An effective restriction scheme could presumably have been established—there were no special difficulties in organising a scheme in this industry—but the producers did not feel it was worth the trouble and risk. On the other hand, the tea industry thought that on balance it was, and so did the lead and zinc industries, though difficulties of organisation and operation are so formidable that the degree of control is far from being as effective as it might be. And these difficulties of organisation and operation are mainly responsible for the absence of restriction schemes in the other industries, such as meat and dairy products, natural silk, etc., in which the position is that they "would if they could, but they can't". Thus the absence of restriction schemes which would be sound according to our analysis, is not due to fundamental faults in that analysis, but either to the fact that, though sound, they may not be deemed expedient or worth while, or to the practical impossibility of making them sufficiently effective.

Now let us turn to the restriction schemes which have been so widely established in industries suffering from excess capacity as well as a temporary decline in the demand, despite the fact that, according to our analysis, restriction schemes in such circumstances are to be condemned. One can of course understand why the high-cost producers in these industries have supported restriction, but why have their low-cost competitors done so, and why have governments been so short-sighted as to lend their powerful support to such unsound schemes? Is it that the whole world is deceiving itself, or allowing itself to be deceived, by the high-cost producers who alone in our view have something to gain? Or is it that our analysis is at fault?

Let us re-examine the point of view of the low-cost producers. When the trade depression begins to make itself felt, and the demand begins to decline, the price of the product usually falls fairly abruptly to a level which is not far above the direct or prime costs of the least efficient producers, prime costs being those costs which vary with the rate of output, and for which money must be found, such as wages, as distinct from the overhead or secondary costs like depreciation and obsolescence, which remain much the same whether the plant is idle or producing at full capacity, but need not be continuously provided for. The price falls nearly to prime costs, because producers will prefer to go on producing so long as they can get some contribution, however small, towards their overhead costs, rather than cease production altogether and have to meet those costs in full. Now a price which will cover the prime costs of the least efficient producers, will probably cover the whole or a large proportion of the total costs (prime and secondary) of the most efficient producers, and therefore the latter are for a time against any resort to restriction, because they hope that, at the now relatively low level of prices, the surplus high-cost capacity will soon be forced to stop production, and perhaps to close down altogether. But as time goes on, the fall in the demand becomes greater, and so far from the total supply being diminished by the closing-down of the highest-cost producers, it very likely increases, because these highest-cost producers will try to increase their output to the utmost possible extent in order to cover their costs or to diminish their actual losses. Hence the price goes on falling lower and lower. But even so there is little sign of the closing-down of capacity, for the highest-cost producers will now be doing everything in their power to reduce even their prime costs. In most agricultural and mining industries wages form a very large proportion of prime costs, far larger than is usually the case in manu-facturing industries where the cost of raw materials is often also a big item, and since there is little chance of getting employment in other industries, seeing that in a world depression all are likely to be more or less depressed, and since in a good many countries pro-ducing primary products there are no other important industries, labour is forced to accept the most severe reductions in wages, perhaps to half the previous level, or even less. In the primary industries prime costs are by no means a fixed minimum: on the contrary they can be very greatly reduced under the spur of necessity, mainly by reducing wages, but also in many other minor ways. So as the price falls, costs also fall, and it may be that even the most efficient producers are unable to cover any appreciable part of their secondary or overhead costs, and still there is little sign that their higher-cost competitors are breaking under the strain. The low-cost producers of course realise that they will be able to stand the strain longest, and that in due course the high-cost producers must give in, but they begin to feel that the game is not worth the candle, and that the fight had better be postponed until it can take place under more favourable circumstances. And in this connection they may reflect that if the fight takes place when general recovery from the world depression is well under way, the elimination of the high-cost producers may well be a much easier process, for, if other industries are expanding, labour will not accept such slashing wage reductions, while the high-cost producers will be in a better position to transfer any of their remaining assets and resources of managerial personnel to some other line of production, and therefore will not hold on so desperately. In short, a period of reasonable and growing general prosperity seems a much more favourable time for the low-cost producers to oust their high-cost competitors than during the worst phases of an acute general trade depression, because the price will not have to fall nearly so low. Consequently the low-cost producers come to agree to the restriction scheme for which the high-cost producers have been pressing all the time. From the former's point of view it means the postponement of the fight until a more favourable occasion; from the latter's point of view it is a life-line which will at least enable them to keep afloat a little longer.

The attitude of the governments of the producing countries must now be considered. This will usually tend to follow the attitude of the majority of their producers: thus if the industry in a particular country is largely composed of high-cost producers, the government will naturally be strongly in favour of a restriction scheme, while if its producers are low-cost, the government will at first be unfavourable, but will change its views as the producers change theirs, if only on the argument that they must know best what is in their own interests as low-cost producers, and that therefore this will be in the interests of the country as a whole. But, in addition, most governments will be predisposed towards restriction during a world trade depression, because they will be face to face with innumerable difficulties of national finance, foreign balances, unemployment and so on, and anything which relieves their present difficulties will seem desirable, even though it may create further difficulties ahead: even if the same government is likely to have to deal with these further difficulties, its members will feel that the future cannot be worse than the present, and may be better. Consequently in a country whose industry includes both high-cost and low-cost producers, the government is in general likely to take sides with the high-cost party in favour of restriction, and even to coerce the low-cost party if its conversion to restriction is unduly delayed. And though this attitude is doubtless usually based on blind instinct, it is all the same a sound attitude, if we accept the reasoning that the elimination of excess high-cost capacity can be achieved with less general economic dislocation, loss and suffering in times of growing general trade activity than in the depths of a general trade depression.

Is this, then, a sound conclusion or not? There is

no easy, certain, and comprehensive answer to this question, straightforward though it seems, for obviously much depends upon the particular circumstances of place and time. But in general there can be little doubt that it is a sound conclusion. On abstract grounds there is a strong common-sense presumption that a transference of resources will be easier when most other industries are active and expanding than when they are depressed and temporarily contracting. Moreover, the experience of the last five years supplies a great deal of evidence that high-cost producers, especially in the primary industries, can put up a tremendous fight for life, and that it needs a much longer period of far lower prices before they give up the struggle than most people used to imagine. On the other hand, we must of course admit that if prices fall below even the lowest level to which the less efficient producers can reduce their prime costs, and remain there, then ultimately these producers will be eliminated, at any rate temporarily, and probably in practice permanently. But again we now know that this process will involve a strain on even the lowest-cost producers so great as to involve them in most serious losses, and perhaps to cripple them more or less permanently. The difficulty is that past records concerning primary industries are not sufficiently detailed to tell us definitely, and in detail, whether excess capacity on the sort of scale which now rules in sugar, rubber, copper or tin, or even wheat or cotton, does get eliminated with comparative ease during periods of general trade recovery, or, in other words, whether the requisite transference is or is not relatively easier then than in times of acute general depression. In the past there do not in fact seem to have been many cases of excess capacity on the same large scale, or of the same type, as have developed in so many primary industries during the last ten years, though this is probably because the economic records of the past are so incomplete. We cannot therefore as yet support our answer by an appeal to actual experience; it must remain a general presumption, though we may hope to collect such experience during the next few years.

Provisionally, however, we must revise our views as to the validity of restriction, even when the troubles of the industry arise not only from a temporary decline in the demand due to a general world depression, but also from capacity in excess of even the normal demand. But we must be careful to accompany our approval by drawing attention to the fact that restriction under such circumstances will no longer be justified when recovery from the general depression gets fairly under way. For then conditions become favourable for the relatively easy elimination of the surplus capacity, and the industry can never regain any true equilibrium until this has been achieved. Now if the low-cost producers can withdraw from the scheme at reasonably short notice, they can probably be relied upon to do so when the best moment for their struggle with the high-cost producers arrives. And as long as this happens, all is well from the consumers' point of view also, since their interests coincide with the low-cost producers' interests. But if the agreement is for a long period, and cannot be abrogated until after the right time has arrived, the low-cost producers will have made an unwise arrangement from their point of view, while consumers will be paying for the continued maintenance of unwanted capacity which can now be eliminated under the most favourable conditions. But a still more serious position is likely to arise if the agreement is not between producers but between their governments. For if the economic situation of a country is improving with the general recovery of world trade, and if the demand for the restricted product is also increasing, so that it appears as if the restriction scheme is over the worst difficulties, and on the way to a successful and triumphant conclusion, the government of that country will be strongly inclined to continue what appears to be a success, and strongly disinclined to risk creating new difficulties for itself by allowing the restriction scheme to come to an end. Even if the national industry is composed of low-cost producers, who now desire the scheme to end, it may well be that their government will be opposed to such desires simply for the sake of immediate peace and quiet, or under the delusion that restriction is curing the troubles of the industry. The government may therefore renew its agreement with the other governments concerned, even though its producers consider that the time is ripe for the elimination of their high-cost competitors. It should be made clear that again we have insufficient practical experience of the ways of governments in such circumstances, but we know only too well that modern governments are prone to take the short view, and to base their policies on the dictates of immediate expediency. The probability is of course stronger still where a government controls both high-cost and low-cost producers: the high-cost producers will naturally favour the continuance of restriction, and the government will almost certainly tend to side with them: while a government which controls only high-cost producers will inevitably do so. Moreover, there is always the possibility that the government may desire to please other governments by agreeing to the continuation of the scheme, and will therefore deliberately sacrifice the best interests of the particular industry concerned, in return for some entirely different political, financial, or economic advantage. Thus, though there is a general presumption that restriction agreements between producers, provided they are of relatively short duration, will be brought to an end by the low-cost producers' opposition to renewal when general recovery is under way, and therefore at the moment which serves the interests of the consumers as well as the long-period interests of the industry, there is no such presumption that this will happen if the agreement is between governments.

The restriction schemes which have been in operation since 1929–30 in such industries as sugar, rubber and tin, where the problem of a temporary decline in the demand due to the world depression was superimposed upon an already existing problem of excess high-cost capacity, may therefore be considered sound in principle, and equally therefore there can be no objection to the participation and support of the governments concerned in the early stages, in order that the schemes might be established on a more solid and comprehensive basis, and might operate more efficiently. The only criticism thus far is that restriction ought in many cases to have been effectively established, or re-established, much earlier, for then the additional problems created by vast accumulated stocks would have been non-existent, or at least much less serious. As regards the operation of the schemes to date, serious criticism may be levelled at the price policy pursued by the more successful schemes. Obviously the consumer ought not to pay a price under restriction higher than is necessary to maintain in efficient working order that proportion of the capacity which he will require in the future. This price will not cover the full costs of the excess high-cost capacity, and there is no reason why the consumer should pay for the full maintenance, depreciation, etc., of capacity which he will never require: if some of this excess high-cost capacity is lost during the restriction scheme, so much the better. Here is a real practical difficulty, however, if the restriction scheme is a voluntary agreement between the producers themselves. For the high-cost producers will naturally do their utmost to force the price to a point where they can earn profits, and the average-cost producers and even the low-cost, having convinced themselves that restriction is necessary and desirable, will find it very difficult to refuse the chance of making substantial profits, even though the excess high-cost producers will thus be able to strengthen their position, and the fight, when it comes, will be all the more severe. Nearly all the available evidence, unfortunately, supports the fear that if a restriction scheme is successful, the price will be raised far higher than is necessary from the consumers' point of view, or desirable in the long-run interests of the industry. This ought to be a further important justification for the participation of governments, for if the scheme is government controlled, the governments can control the price. In fact, governments seem to be as bad as, or worse than, the producers when left to themselves, as witness the recent history of the tin restriction scheme; and government schemes have usually greater monopolistic power than private schemes. In addition, there is the fear that governments will not bring restriction to an end at the proper moment, but will tend to postpone indefinitely the admittedly difficult process involved in the elimination of surplus high-cost capacity, thus continuing a burden on the consumer which has become wholly unjustifiable, and probably jeopardising the future prosperity of the industry as a whole. Yet the inference that governments ought not under any circumstances to take a hand in restriction schemes is emphatically to be resisted. Under certain conditions restriction is economically sound, and offers great potential advantages over *laissez-faire*. But in many industries government assistance and control is necessary for the efficient operation and administration of the scheme, and governments have the power to see that the scheme is so conducted as to serve the long-period interests of the industry and therefore of the consumers. To prohibit government participation because, at the present time, governments are imperfectly aware of their responsibilities, or cannot be trusted to use their powers properly, is a deplorable counsel of despair. The correct inference is that governments must learn as quickly as possible how to play their proper part in this new form of industrial organisation with which the world is experimenting on such a wide scale.

As the result of this rather protracted, because intricate, study of the economics of restriction in times of world trade depression, we can therefore add two further conclusions to the three which appear at the beginning of this chapter concerning restriction in times of world trade prosperity. But as these five conclusions in part overlap and involve duplication, for example in respect of a temporary decline in demand, it will be convenient to present a consolidated statement.

(1) Restriction is economically *unsound* as a means of meeting a permanent decline in the demand for the product of a particular industry during times of general prosperity, and is more than likely to intensify the difficulties of the inevitable readjustment of resources; but in times of general depression it may be justifiable until general recovery is under way, since in the depths

of a depression the readjustment of resources will probably present the maximum of difficulty. (We have not in fact considered the case of a permanent decline of demand in times of general depression, but the above conclusion clearly follows from our discussion about excess capacity. It may be observed that this condemnation of restriction as a cure for the trouble created by a permanent decline in the demand, does not imply that *laissez-faire* is the best cure; that form of artificial control usually known as rationalisation may be better than *laissez-faire*, but this is a matter outside the scope of this book.)

(2) Restriction is economically *sound*, as a means of meeting a temporary decline in the demand for the product of a particular industry, both during times of general prosperity and of general depression, provided that no substantial proportion of the productive capacity is in an advanced stage of obsolescence, this proviso being of special importance if there is any tendency towards excess capacity before the demand declines.

(3) Restriction can at no time be a cure for troubles arising from excessive capacity, unless the productive technique of the industry in the widest sense of that term is virtually stationary—a condition which is nowadays most unlikely to be fulfilled. In times of general prosperity, a resort to restriction where this condition is not fulfilled will be useless, and is extremely liable to make the necessary readjustments still more difficult. But in times of general depression, the difficulties of readjustment are at a maximum and

therefore a restriction scheme may be legitimately used, as a means of postponing such readjustment until general trade recovery is sufficiently far advanced to minimise the loss and dislocation inevitably involved.

There is little more that need be said concerning the application of these conclusions to existing restriction schemes. It is hardly an exaggeration to say that at the present time the general view of producers and their governments is that restriction is a panacea for all ills, to be applied indiscriminately in all ways which seem to offer a momentary advantage, irrespective of the possibly disastrous results in the near or more distant future: while for the same reason the consumers' point of view is entirely neglected. The truth is that restriction is an extremely powerful drug, which in wise and discriminating hands can be used to effect great improvements in the world's economic organisation: but if used as a panacea, it will certainly bring some patients near to death, even though it will naturally by chance assist others. We do not yet fully know when, how and in what doses this drug should be used, but it is virtually certain that it is no panacea, that there are some circumstances in which it is deadly dangerous, and others in which it is likely to be beneficial if carefully administered. If governments wish or are forced to play the role of economic doctor, the sooner they learn what can at present be learned about the use of restriction, the better it will be for their patients, both producers and consumers; and the same is true if the producers wish to doctor themselves.

Chapter XI

THE ECONOMICS OF VALORISATION SCHEMES

A. Valorisation Schemes for Single Crops

IN the two previous chapters we have been concerned with artificial control schemes involving
restrictions on output, but we must not forget the
other main category of control schemes, commonly
called valorisation schemes. Such schemes have never
been so widespread or of such general importance, and
their scope is in any case limited to commodities which
are produced in an annual crop and/or the crop yield
of which is greatly affected by weather conditions. But
since both these conditions apply to such staple
agricultural crops as wheat, cotton and coffee, and to
many other less important crops in varying degrees,
the question whether valorisation does or does not
offer possibilities of improvement as compared with
laissez-faire is of very great importance, and certainly
demands our most careful attention.

The use of the word valorisation is in some ways
unfortunate, for it may be taken to mean the valorisation of the price of the product, and then all restriction
schemes might be termed valorisation schemes. Unfortunately the word is sometimes so used, but it has
acquired a definitely technical application in connection
with artificial control schemes, as meaning the valorisation of producers' incomes, not through a raising of

prices above the level at which the current demand and supply are in equilibrium by restricting the total amount of the available supply, but by regulating the flow of the available supply to the market so as to stabilise the price at the long-period, or normal equilibrium, level, thus preventing the sharp downward fluctuations of the price which accompany a temporary excess of supplies, and the sharp upward fluctuations which accompany a temporary shortage. In other words, the essence of a valorisation scheme, in the technical sense of the word, is the regulation of the flow of available supplies to the market *through some period of time*, whereas the essence of a restriction scheme is the limitation of available supplies for a period of time to a level below what they would otherwise be. If a valorisation scheme is started in a period of temporary glut, when the price is below the long-period or normal level, then the object of the scheme is to raise the price to that level by withholding part of the existing supplies from the market; but this is only a necessary first step, and when the price has reached that level, any further rise, due to a possible temporary shortage of current new supplies, will be prevented by releasing the accumulated stocks. Thus, though the initial objective of a valorisation scheme may be similar to that of a restriction scheme, this is merely because the former happens to have been initiated at a particular time: if it had been initiated when the price was in equilibrium, there would be no raising of prices, but the objective would be to maintain that price-level by regulating the flow of available supplies to the market as and when necessary.

Now there are two main kinds of valorisation schemes, those which are confined to regulating the available supply over a single crop year, and those which aim at regulating the available supplies over more than one crop year, or permanently. The latter type is obviously the more ambitious and the more important, and when one speaks of a valorisation scheme, one normally refers to this latter type. But the regularisation of the flow of a single crop to the market is not to be confused with schemes for collective marketing such as are so much to the fore in English agriculture to-day—a "marketing scheme" does not necessarily include arrangements for regulating the available supply over the crop year; if it does, it becomes also a valorisation scheme restricted to that single year. Before we study valorisation schemes extending over several years, it is desirable therefore to pay some attention to those restricted to a single year.

With many annual crops, such as wheat and cotton, a substantial proportion of the producers possess insufficient working capital, and in order to pay for the heavy expenses of harvesting, they are virtually forced to sell their crop, or a large part of it, at the earliest possible moment. Consequently, directly after the harvest, too large a proportion of the whole crop is offered for sale, and the price tends to fall in order to induce merchant-speculators to buy what they know they will have to store until later in the season. During the storage interval the merchant-speculator has to incur not only the costs of the actual storage operations (i.e. rent of warehouse, extra handling costs, damage by weather and vermin, etc., which in all total an appreciable amount), but also the interest charge on the capital locked up by his purchase. Thus, to induce merchant-speculators to buy up that part of the supplies on offer in the market which is not required for current consumption and must therefore be stored for a time, the price often falls very considerably in the weeks following the close of the harvest, and those producers who must sell in order to get cash for the payment of pressing obligations, suffer accordingly. Even if they sell only a part of their crop, they will not recoup themselves when they sell the remainder later in the season, for the price will not rise above the equilibrium or true level for the crop as a whole during that crop year, because, though producers will be selling less than is currently demanded, the merchant-speculators will be selling off what they have bought earlier in the season and have been holding in store. Thus, from the producers' point of view, their need for cash drives them to sell at less than the true equilibrium price, and the merchant-speculator makes profits at their expense. If the available supply could be put on the market regularly throughout the season, producers would get more for their crop by an amount representing the merchant-speculators' profits, and possibly more still, by reason of the producers being able to store what has to be stored more cheaply.[1]

[1] On this matter, see pp. 247–248.

One solution of this problem of seasonal selling pressure after the harvest lies along the lines of organising the cheapest possible credit supplies for the producer in order to make forced sales of his crop unnecessary. This may be done and has been done, in various ways, but the two fundamental principles are either through the organisation of the producers into a co-operative body which obtains credit from commercial banks on the security of the members' combined resources of all kinds, including perhaps the pledging of a percentage of each member's crop, or through the establishment of a state bank or government department, which can lend at low rates of interest because the credit of the country has been used to provide its capital at relatively low rates. Such measures may do a good deal in the direction of obviating distress sales, but they do not ensure that the crop will be brought to market regularly throughout the season; on the contrary, they are quite likely to result in even greater irregularity than that which arises simply from the evil which such measures are intended to cure. For if individual producers are armed with the ability to withhold supplies for a time, they will almost certainly "take a view of the market", that is they will try to sell at something better than the equilibrium price for the crop as a whole over the year. Now if the individual producer had the facilities and the experience to make a carefully reasoned study of the conditions of supply and demand, then, over any given time, say a month, some would decide to sell more and others less than the due and proper proportion of their crop, and on balance the supply would be about right. But in industries where there are many relatively small-scale producers, such as wheat, or cotton, or even coffee, the producers have inadequate facilities for the study of world conditions of supply and demand, and therefore they naturally have not got the experience. The result is that they all tend to follow each other like a flock of sheep. Word goes round that Farmer X., whose shrewdness is considered to be above the average, has sold his crop; all who hear it, proceed to do the same, and there is a glut of supplies. Or rumour goes round that the price which seems low at the moment will be much higher in three months' time; every producer holds back his supplies, and there is a shortage, which certainly tends to put the price up while it lasts, but cannot result in a higher average price if the rumour was based on false expectations. Thus the cure of cheap credit facilities is apt to produce greater irregularity in the flow of supplies and more harm to the producer than the particular irregularity which it remedies.

Consequently valorisation to be effective must usually involve collective instead of individual selling. The producers form a pool or co-operative selling organisation, and agree to deliver to it the whole of their crop; the pool then sells what it sees fit to sell, and uses the proceeds of these sales to make an advance to the producers on their whole crop, thus enabling them to meet their most pressing expenses for the harvesting just completed, or for preparing the ground for the new crop. At the end of the season, or when the whole crop is sold, the pool shares out the balance after paying all expenses incurred, allowances being made according to the quality of each producer's crop, and so on. Thus the pool can regulate the flow of the crop to the market over the crop year as a whole, temporary falls in the price owing to forced sales are avoided, and the producer gets the full proper equilibrium price for his crop.

So described, the operations of such pools appear simple. Actually there is no such simplicity, for the only simple method of regulating the flow of supplies to the market, namely to divide the crop by the number of days on which the market is open during the year and sell that amount each day, is certainly not going to stabilise the price, and almost certainly the average price so obtained will be much below the true equilibrium price. It is not going to stabilise the price because in fact buyers do not want supplies with such mechanical regularity. In the first place, the final consumer does not even buy all foodstuffs absolutely regularly throughout the year, and buys manufactures still less regularly, owing to the general social customs and procedure which have arisen as the result of climatic seasonal changes, changes in fashion, and the modern organisation of retailing. For this reason, though manufacturers and processers would like to operate their plants regularly throughout the year, they can rarely do so, and their demand for raw foodstuffs and materials tends to vary seasonally, while shipping conditions, both climatic and economic, may provoke additional variations. Again, manufacturers and processers may consider it a legitimate part of their business to buy speculatively, and not merely in line with their current or anticipated rate of absorption, while in any case merchant-speculators will be buying or selling in accordance with their anticipations as to changes in the trend of the demand for the particular commodity. Hence, though the supply would be regularised on this mechanical basis, the demand would remain irregular, and consequently prices would fluctuate day by day, week by week and month by month. Such price fluctuation will inevitably give rise to discontent amongst the producers, who will complain that their pool manager must be an idiot to press supplies on to the market on the days or during the period when demand was obviously below normal; and the pool manager's retort, that what is lost by low prices on such days must be gained by correspondingly higher than normal prices on the days when demand is above normal, and that such days must come some time during the year, does not carry conviction, even though it appears so logical. Consequently the fact of such price fluctuations tends to create discontent and dissatisfaction among the members of the pool, and to lead to a demand for more intelligent, that is, unmechanical and therefore speculative, selling policies.

But this is not all the story. The pool manager's retort outlined above is only really true if the conditions of the market remain strictly competitive on the buyers' side. In fact mechanical selling of this character simply invites combination amongst buyers in order to obtain the fixed daily, weekly or monthly supply at a merely nominal price, and then share it out amongst the members of the combination. Though a complete combination would rarely be practicable, much might be done by a combination covering directly or indirectly a large proportion of the regular users of the product, or even of the regular established merchant firms. Such combination amongst the buyers would almost certainly be evolved sooner or later, and then the average price obtained by the producers' selling organisation might be much below the true equilibrium level. Thus a mechanical selling policy is really not practical politics.

The alternative policy is to sell each day, week or month, what can be sold without depressing the price below what the pool managers estimate to be its proper equilibrium level over the season. This means, of course, that everything will depend upon the accuracy of their estimates of demand over the season as a whole, and unless the pool covers all who sell on the world market, it may also depend on estimates of the volume of "outside" production. As compared with an individual merchant-speculator, the pool managers will usually, of course, be in a better position to make such estimates, but there must inevitably be a large element of guesswork, and the pool managers, ever mindful of the opinions of the members, will naturally tend to take an optimistic rather than a pessimistic view of developments during the year; they will, for example, be apt to interpret a tendency for prices to fall as a mere temporary postponement of purchases, and so hold back supplies, when the truth is that the demand, and therefore the equilibrium price, is falling to lower levels for a considerable period. In short, they will naturally tend to resist any fall in price, while they may find it equally hard to resist the temptation to exploit a rise in prices above what they believe to be the equilibrium level. One way or another, and sooner or later, it is almost certain that an abnormally large amount will be carried over into the next crop year, even though the pool managers are really able and experienced men, whose sole aim is to sell the crop at the best price it will fetch during the year. Moreover if the pool has to face a permanent decline in the price, due either to a permanent contraction in the demand, or to an over-expansion of capacity, or to a reduction in costs as the result of improved technique, dissatisfaction amongst the members as a whole, or at least amongst the higher-cost section, may virtually compel the pool managers deliberately to go against their own judgment of the situation, and to hold back supplies in the hope that conditions will improve in the near future. Once surplus stocks have accumulated, the pool will be face to face with ever-growing difficulties, both in its actual selling operations (for the weakness of its position cannot for long be hidden from buyers) and in its relations with its members. Nothing but extremely strong, and therefore most unpopular, measures, or a great stroke of luck, will then extricate the pool from its difficulties.

The truth of this analysis of the difficulties of even single-crop valorisation schemes is amply borne out by the history of the Canadian wheat pools, and of the cotton co-operative associations in the United States. The wheat pools started out with the sole intention of regulating the flow of each crop to the market, and so preventing the seasonal price-fall in the autumn, due to sales forced by the producers' need for cash. For several years all went relatively well, and the membership of the pools so greatly increased that by 1926 they had a considerable measure of monopolistic power at least in the Canadian market. But surplus stocks were slowly accumulating, and even the prospect of a huge bumper crop in 1928 was not sufficient to convince the pools of the desirability, and indeed the common sense, of reducing the carry-over from the previous year to the smallest possible dimensions, even if this involved the acceptance of low prices. When the great bumper crop had been harvested, the pools could not escape the popular delusion in North America during the autumn of 1928, that there would be no great difficulty in disposing of the crop, that buyers were wrong in thinking the contrary, and that in the spring their accumulated orders would carry the price much higher. So the pools refused to sell except at a price which would have been reasonable if the crop had been normal or rather less than normal, but which under the circumstances failed to tempt buyers. In the spring, the great increase in buying failed to materialise, and, as we know, things went from bad to worse, and then became desperate. This is of course a very summary account, and neglects many other factors which were in operation, but the essence of the situation was as described.

The tale of the early history of the cotton co-operatives is very similar, and need not be repeated here. These are perhaps the most important examples of single-crop valorisation schemes, but the experience of several smaller schemes all goes to confirm the conclusion that the regulation of the flow of a crop to market over the crop year is a much more difficult problem than might be supposed by the uninitiated. Mechanical selling arrangements are impossible; some element of speculation on the part of the producers' organisation is inevitable; and sooner or later this will lead to trouble. There is no means of determining whether on balance such valorisation schemes will, or will not, benefit the producers in comparison with the merchant-speculator regime of *laissez-faire*, since everything depends on the skill with which the pool managers execute their task. It may be observed that the more complete, up-to-date and reliable the statistical information of the pool becomes, the more accurate should its estimates and speculations become; improvement in this direction probably will take place naturally, and may easily be assisted artificially. Probably producers will continue such experiments in artificial control, and if they will learn two lessons, such experiments may well prove advantageous and not too costly. The first is the danger of expecting too much, and so increasing the natural over-optimism of the managers of their organisation in respect of market conditions and prices; and the second is that if things begin to go wrong and surplus stocks accumulate, it is better to get rid of them at once, no matter what the cost involved, rather than to attempt an inevitably protracted cure.

B. Valorisation Schemes for Crop Cycles

We now turn to valorisation schemes extending over several crop years. The aim of such schemes is to neutralise the effects of weather variations on the size of successive crops by regulating the flow of supplies to the market, holding back the surplus of bumper crops until the corresponding short crops occur. The general weather conditions in any particular region of the world are of course changing, or liable to be changing, all the time, but such changes are usually very slow—an affair of centuries. Thus for practical purposes we can more or less legitimately talk of the average or normal weather conditions of a region, meaning that the temperature, rainfall and so on, over any selected period of a few years, will average out relatively near the average of any other selected period of about the same length. In some parts of the earth the number of years required to give roughly similar average figures is much smaller than in other parts, but usually between five and ten years will be sufficient, and we can then loosely designate this period as the weather cycle of the particular region. Within this cycle there may of course be very great differences between one year and another, and in some years the conditions will be specially favourable to a particular crop, and in others specially unfavourable. But as the weather averages out over the cycle, so will the crops average out, and therefore we can also loosely speak of a crop cycle. Under conditions of *laissez-faire*, producers sell their crops to merchants, who usually store part, though not the whole, of the excess of a bumper crop until a correspondingly short crop occurs. The aim of crop-cycle valorisation schemes is so to regulate the flow of supplies to the market that each year an amount roughly equal to the average crop of the cycle is offered for sale, the excess of any crop being stored until it is required, not by merchants, but by the producers themselves.

The most important and the most continuous series of experiments in this kind of valorisation has been with Brazilian coffee, and it will perhaps be simplest to consider the case for valorisation in terms of Brazilian coffee, though we must not forget that we are considering a rather special case with marked characteristics of its own. For the Brazilian coffee-crop cycle is not simply a Brazilian weather cycle, but a compound of this and a cycle peculiar to the coffee tree itself. As was explained in chapter II, particularly good weather results in a bumper crop, but the bearing of that bumper crop so exhausts the vitality of the trees that however good the weather during the following season, there could not be a second bumper crop that next year, and normally the trees are not in a condition to bear another such crop for three or four years. After that, the bumper crop may come at any time, depending entirely on the weather. Thus on the whole the coffee-tree cycle is more marked than the weather cycle, even though the bumper crop itself is produced solely by the weather, and there is therefore a much higher degree of certainty that a bumper crop will be balanced by short crops within a relatively short period of three or four years than in most commodities, where two successive bumper crops are by no means impossible, and several average crops may occur before the corresponding short crops.

Summarising the case for valorisation which has already been presented in chapter II, the reader may be reminded that the fundamental issue, from the coffee producers' point of view, was that when a bumper crop occurred, the price obtainable by them was far below the price appropriate to an average crop, but that when the corresponding short crop or crops came along, the price did not rise above the average level because the merchants had stored most of the excess of the bumper crop, and now added these stocks to the deficient new crop, thus bringing the total supply available up to normal, that is average, dimensions—the consumer of course paid roughly the normal price in the bumper year as well as in the short year, and the merchant made his expenses of storage and his profits out of the difference between the low price which he paid to the producer for the bumper crop and the normal price which he obtained from the consumer. The

Brazilian producers therefore argued that if they held back the excess of the bumper crop from the market until the short crop occurred, they would get the normal price for both bumper and short crops, less any costs which they had incurred in holding the excess. Over and above the mere costs of warehousing, depreciation, etc., which may be termed the physical costs of storage, as distinct from the interest charges which may be termed the financial costs, some additional cost would be involved, because the receipts in the bumper year from selling only that part of the crop which was equal to an average crop, would probably not cover the abnormally great total costs incurred in producing and harvesting that bumper crop. The producers would therefore have to borrow in order to obtain cash for their pressing expenses. As a result of the variation in the crops, their profits, over the cycle, would be less by the physical costs of storing the excess of the bumper crop, together with a substantial interest charge on what they would have to borrow. But it was argued that this loss of profits would be very much less than the loss incurred under the merchant-speculator regime of *laissez-faire*.

This argument seems to suggest that producers receive less than normal profits over each and every crop cycle. By "normal profits" is usually meant such a rate of return to capital and enterprise as will maintain the existing volume of production but not increase it. On the basis of this definition, the above argument is nonsense, because if normal profits are not earned in the long run, the industry will contract, supplies will decrease, and the price will rise until the remaining producers do receive adequate, that is, normal profits. The truth must obviously be that on average crops the producers' profits must be sufficient to offset the loss which is certainly incurred when crops are above or below the average. It seems therefore that, provided producers pursue a proper financial policy, putting aside reserves in average crop years wherewith to meet the losses incurred when their crops vary, all is well, and they have no real cause of complaint and no right to any more profits than they are getting: indeed, if they succeed by a valorisation scheme in getting more profits, the result will be to stimulate the establishment of new additional capacity which will lower the average price, and so the industry will contract again to its former dimensions. In short, though, admittedly, producers make less profits over a cycle of varying crops than they would do if the crops did not vary, it does not follow that they make less than the long-period normal rate of profits appropriate when the crops do vary. The producer bears the costs arising from crop variations in the first instance and in the short run, but the consumer pays in the long run, because the long-run average price is higher than it would be in the absence of crop variations to the extent necessary to give producers normal profits in the long run, and so induce them to maintain the existing volume of production. It seems therefore that crop variations do not really give rise to any grievance from the producers' point of view, because they are simply one of the risks inherent in the industry, of which producers are well aware, and for which they get proper compensation. Any change in the existing method of regulating supplies through a merchant-speculator regime is really not a producer's problem at all, but a consumer's problem, since the only real issue is whether a change of system will reduce the real cost arising from crop variations, and will therefore reduce the average long-period price which the consumer has to pay for his supply of the particular commodity.

In theory there does not seem to be much wrong. But in practice the story usually runs rather differently. In the first place, this theory demands that producers should have considerable reserves of working capital so that they may be able to withstand the losses incurred by abnormal crops, if such crops occur before a succession of average crops has enabled them to build up reserves. But we know that in many primary industries, the whole or part of the producing units are not organised on what may be briefly termed a capitalist basis, but consist of natives, peasant proprietors, and men in a small way of business, all of whom are usually mortgaged up to the hilt in return for a working capital which is usually much below the amount required for producing even an average crop. Much the same is often true of relatively large-scale joint-stock enterprises. In the second place, it seems most unlikely that the long-period average price is above the costs of a normal crop to the extent required to make good the producers' losses on abnormal crops. Large numbers of producers almost certainly underestimate or ignore the risks arising from crop variations: they do not—and for practical purposes one must say that they cannot—take a sufficiently long view in determining whether or no the current price of a normal crop exceeds the costs of that normal crop by the margin required to make good the inevitable losses on abnormal crops. Such producers enter the industry if they reckon they can make a profit on a normal crop at the current price. They have no reserves, and therefore really abnormal crops mean disaster. The theorist may reply that they are fools, and as such should be punished for their folly. But this does not alter the fact that they have invested their capital and their enterprise in the industry, and therefore it seems to them intolerable that merchant-speculators should be making profits out of circumstances which to them spell ruin. A system which depends upon the smooth working of long-period adjustments is not a system which is likely to seem satisfactory to those who, whether in ignorance or folly, have taken short-period views. From the producers' point of view, the merchant-speculator regime of *laissez-faire* has the great, the almost intolerable, defect, that the producer has to foot the bill in the first instance, and no amount of argument by the theorist, concerning the long-period ultimate incidence of the costs involved in averaging out supplies over crop cycles, is likely to convince him that this regime is fair and the best possible. Thus, in practice, crop variations do present a real problem from the producer's point of view, and he will therefore try to solve this problem either along the lines of shifting the first incidence of the costs involved off his own shoulders, and/or of reducing the actual amount of these costs.

The argument of our Brazilian coffee growers, as presented above, is not therefore based on sheer delusion, and we must proceed to examine their claim that the loss of profits under a valorisation scheme in which the producers themselves carry over the excess of a bumper crop until the occurrence of the corresponding short crop or crops, will be very much less than the loss incurred under the merchant-speculator regime of *laissez-faire*. Now it may be argued that competition amongst merchants will ensure that the function of equalising supplies is performed by the merchant-speculator regime at the least possible cost, and that therefore the producers will get the highest average price which is economically possible. That competition usually rules under the merchant-speculator regime is a fact which cannot be denied, for the supply of merchant-speculators is limited only by the opportunity of making profits. But the idea that this ensures that the job of equalising supplies will be done at the least possible cost does not necessarily follow.

At first sight, however, there may seem little reason to suppose that the producers as a body can perform the function more cheaply than merchant-speculators.

Suppose, for example, the producers' organisation proceeds to buy up the excess of the bumper crop in the open market, just as in the same way the merchants do at present. They must borrow money, for the members will have no capital to subscribe, and though theoretically if the organisation is a strong one, and if the members pledge all their assets as security, they should be able to borrow more cheaply than individual merchants can do, in practice this is not very likely, since at any rate, at the beginning, the producers' organisation will not command the unquestioning respect and confidence of the world's financiers as to the ability and integrity of its leaders or the soundness of their policy, and the collateral assets which the members can offer will not be of a very liquid and therefore attractive character, while in only too many cases these assets will have already been mortgaged up to the hilt. And if they could borrow merely on the same terms as the merchant, there would be no advantage, for they would require exactly the same amount, while of course the physical costs of storage would be the same. The only practical hope of cheaper borrowing would be if the producers' government guaranteed the loan, or better still if the producers' government took over the whole administration, and itself supplied or borrowed the necessary finance. Even countries of primary production, in their earliest stages of development, can usually borrow at something considerably less than 10 per cent. But governments have usually, and up to the present time, shown considerable reluctance to undertake what is necessarily a risky business, unless the industry concerned is such an important source of the national wealth that the government revenues will be severely depleted if the situation is left to the merchant-speculator. And when governments in this position do undertake the task, they usually want to retain for government purposes every penny that they can make out of the business, so that the producers themselves may be very little better off, even though the costs of the necessary stock-holding have been reduced.

If this were the only alternative open to the producers' organisation, they would probably find themselves little better off, as was indeed the experience of our Brazilian coffee friends whose earlier experiments in valorisation took this form. But the alternative, which was outlined in their name towards the beginning of this section, is entirely different. The proposal there was that in a bumper-crop year the producers should only send to market an amount equal to the estimated average crop of the cycle, and should store the remainder, borrowing such a sum as was necessary in order to enable them to meet the difference between the receipts from what they sold and the total costs of producing and harvesting the bumper crop. The producers will have to borrow, at least in cases where the crop is much above average, because in the coffee industry as in most agricultural industries, the total costs of producing the bumper crop will be considerably above the total costs of producing an average crop, and will amount to more than the selling value of an average crop. Producers do not normally possess a working capital sufficient to finance the production of a bumper crop on the basis of their receipts from the sale of an average crop, and therefore borrowing is inevitable. Under *laissez-faire* no such borrowing will be necessary, because, by selling the whole of a bumper crop, producers' receipts will usually exceed their total expenses, even though the price obtained will be much below normal: but under a valorisation scheme, even though they sell the equivalent of an average crop at the equilibrium price, some borrowing will usually be required. Thus the costs of a valorisation scheme conducted along these lines will be composed of two parts: (*a*) the physical costs of storing the excess of the bumper crop, and (*b*) the interest charge on what the producers have to borrow in order to meet the difference between their receipts and expenses in the bumper-crop year, which interest charge will continue until the short crop occurs and the excess of the bumper crop can be safely released from storage. How are we to determine whether this combined cost is or is not greater than the loss incurred by the producers under the merchant-speculator regime?

We know that under the merchant-speculator regime producers normally make a profit on the bumper crop, even though the price is relatively low, because their costs per bag or per ton, or whatever is the unit, will be much lower than normal on such a large crop (their total costs for the bumper crop, of which we have hitherto been speaking, will of course be much higher than normal, but the reverse will be true of their unit costs). This profit on the bumper crop is followed in due course by a relatively greater loss on the short crop. The complaint of the producer is not that he makes *no* profits in the bumper year, but that he might have made much bigger profits if the price had not been so absurdly low, and then he would at least have been better able to meet the staggering loss entailed by the short crop. Now it is clear that this profit on the bumper crop is not really a true profit at all: it is a temporary surplus which will be more than offset when the short crop occurs: it is in fact a sort of loan from the merchants to the producers, which competition amongst themselves forces the merchants to give the producers in order that they may induce them to sell the whole crop. Moreover, since merchants have to pay for the use of capital, it is really a loan carrying an interest rate, and a relatively high one because the merchant is using his capital in a rather risky business. Since this surplus or loan will be more than offset by the loss on the short crop when that occurs, obviously the producer must not spend a penny of it: he must put it into absolutely safe keeping so that he can realise it in order to meet his coming losses on the short crop, and if he can make it earn some interest, so much the better, though it may be pointed out that he can never make it earn as much as the merchants are invisibly charging him for it, because he cannot afford to run any risks.

Let us assume for the moment that producers appreciate the true nature of the profits which they appear to make on the bumper crop, and let us then compare the working of the merchant-speculator regime with a valorisation scheme under which the producers themselves retain the excess of a bumper crop. Let us further assume for simplicity that the crop cycle consists of a bumper crop, and one correspondingly short crop. In the bumper-crop year the producers will get a surplus of receipts over expenses under the merchant-speculator regime, whereas under the valorisation scheme they will find that their receipts, from the sale of only that amount of the bumper crop which is equal to the average normal crop, fall short of their total expenses of producing the bumper crop, and so they will have to borrow the difference. When the short crop comes along, the producers will lose under the merchant-speculator regime more than the surplus which they got in the bumper year, whereas under the valorisation scheme they will gain by an amount equal to the sum which they had to borrow in the bumper year. Therefore, over the cycle as a whole, the producers will lose under the merchant-speculator regime by the excess of their losses in the short year over the surplus received in the bumper year, and under the valorisation scheme by the interest charge on the sum borrowed in the bumper year, together with the physical costs of storing the excess of the bumper crop until the short crop arrives. Now assuming, as we have already done, that the producers carefully preserve the surplus which they get in the bumper year under the merchant-speculator regime, and assuming also, for the sake of a direct comparison, that the producers pay the same rate of interest for what they borrow as the merchant-speculators pay for the capital which they use in their operations, and assuming thirdly that the physical storage costs are the same for both producers and merchants, then one would, I think, on general common-sense grounds, expect the producers' loss over the cycle to be very much the same under the merchant-speculator regime and under the valorisation scheme. This can in fact be demonstrated as broadly true under a very wide range of conditions including varying sizes of bumper crops, varying kinds of demand, varying proportions of the items which compose the producers' cost, and so on. But since I know of no way in which this can be simply and neatly demonstrated, I am going to ask the reader to give credit to his general common sense, and leave it at that. Thus on these assumptions it is correct to assert that the merchant-speculator regime performs the equalisation of supplies over a crop cycle at the least possible cost, and that a valorisation scheme of the character which we have been considering cannot be an improvement from the producers', any more than from the consumers', point of view.

Let us however be assured that the assumptions which we have made are legitimate and reasonable. The first was that the producers recognise the true nature of the surplus which they get in the bumper year under the merchant-speculator regime, and will carefully preserve it to help them meet the still greater loss which they know they will suffer in the short-crop year. Now it must be realised that in the real world very few producers will do any such thing. Will the ordinary native producer or smallholder realise that the balance of his receipts over his expenses on the bumper crop is no true profit at all, and will he resolutely refuse to spend a penny of it? Will even the ordinary joint-stock company put its profits on the bumper crop entirely to reserve, and refuse to pay any dividend whatever? No one could answer these questions in the affirmative. What happens in practice is that producers of all kinds, big and small, look upon any surplus in the bumper year as a true profit, which they proceed to spend forthwith, for they never stop to think that sooner or later the bumper crop will be balanced by short crops, or, if they do, they quote with approval that biblical motto which begins, "Take no thought for the morrow ". The big joint-stock company may put something to reserve, but usually not more than it does in a normal year, and the shareholders certainly will not invest their dividends, and so provide personal reserves. The family owners of large sugar estates in Cuba, or of large coffee estates in Brazil, will go to Paris and spend every penny. The small producer of wheat or cotton will do much the same on his lower scale, or else he will buy more land or build a bigger house. The native producer will buy a share in a motor car or perhaps another wife! One thing is certain, namely that the profits of the bumper year will be either spent or turned into nonliquid or absolutely fixed capital. That is the way things work out in the real world, and hence the reason why under the merchant-speculator regime the short crop means such a staggering loss to most producers. Accordingly we must in practice deny that our assumption as to the producers' behaviour is legitimate: it would be far nearer reality to assume that producers dispose irrevocably of every penny of the surplus which they receive in the bumper year. In that case, it is clear that the producers' loss will be much greater under the merchant-speculator regime than under the valorisation scheme. And there is a further gain from the producers' point of view under the valorisation scheme. For in the bumper-crop year the producers have to borrow, and if the borrowing is in fact done by the individual producers, as would normally be the case though perhaps with the assistance of their collective organisation, each producer has to pay interest, and therefore he will have every incentive to cut down both his own living expenses and his current expenses of producing succeeding crops, while joint-stock companies will draw upon their reserves and pay no dividends whatever. This enforced economy does not of course further diminish the real costs under the valorisation scheme, but it does alter their incidence, and in a way which is likely to be beneficial to the producers.

So much for our first assumption. Even if the other two assumptions are legitimate, we must conclude that valorisation will be in practice, though not in theory, a considerable improvement on the merchant-speculator regime from the producers' point of view. This conclusion is reinforced by a brief consideration of the other two assumptions. The second assumption was that the producers have to pay the same rate of interest on what they borrow as the merchant-speculators pay for the capital which they use in their operations. The producers' borrowing will of course be done through their collective organisation. Such an organisation would certainly be able to borrow more cheaply than the ordinary merchant-speculator once its reputation was reasonably well established, and during its early days at least, if the industry were an important national industry, it would probably be able to obtain a guarantee from the government or governments concerned, and thus borrow on very reasonable terms. Whereas a merchant might have to pay around 8–10 per cent. for his capital, the producers might in practice be able to borrow around 5–7 per cent., and this will make a very substantial difference in favour of the valorisation scheme, and one which will ultimately benefit the consumer.

Thirdly, we assumed that the physical storage costs would be the same for the producers' organisation as for the merchant-speculators. Usually the merchant-speculator must make use of existing facilities for warehousing, and these are at the main ports of shipment from the producing country, or at the main ports of consuming areas, and therefore the charges are high because of the high rents, high wage rates, and so on, which are associated with large towns. If the producers' organisation can establish warehouses, at central points up-country, in the actual producing areas—points such as railway junctions—it may be able to warehouse at a much lower cost than is possible at large ports or marketing centres. Incidentally, if that is arranged, it becomes unnecessary that the whole of the bumper crop should be moved right down to the port of shipment as early as possible, and so the peak load of the railways or other transport system need not be so great, and therefore the charges for transport should be reduced. There is certainly scope for economy of the actual physical storage costs by a producers' combine, but even if this possibility is not exploited, the physical storage costs will certainly be no greater than they are for the merchant-speculator. Here again, if this scope for economy is exploited, the consumer will ultimately benefit.

We therefore reach a final conclusion in favour of valorisation schemes as an improvement over the merchant-speculator regime from the producers' point of view, and incidentally also from the point of view of the ultimate interests of consumers: a valorisation scheme of this character not only alters the first incidence of the costs of crop variations, but it is also likely to reduce them. But in pronouncing this judgment, and in recommending producers in industries subject to large crop variations to experiment more freely with this form of artificial control, we should be careful to stress one aspect of the matter in particular.

Clearly if producers borrow more than is strictly necessary for the purpose of bridging the gap between their receipts in the bumper-crop year and the total costs of producing that bumper crop, the advantage of the valorisation scheme as compared with the merchant-speculator regime will be rapidly diminished. It is essential that the producers should not borrow one penny more than is absolutely necessary: the more they borrow, the greater must their losses be, and if they borrow freely, valorisation may easily involve them in even greater losses than does the merchant-speculator regime. Now the trouble is that at present producers' organisations are usually able to borrow far more than they ought to borrow—far more, in other words, than is good for them. For commercial banks are normally prepared to make a loan on the security of stocks of commodities up to 70–80 per cent., and perhaps even more, of the value of the stocks at the current market price. But the bank, as lender, must have evidence that the borrower really has possession of the stocks, and the bank must be able to take over those stocks with reasonable ease and convenience in case of necessity owing to default on the part of the borrower. Therefore banks are not usually willing to lend to producers on the security of stocks stored on the farm or plantation, though they will lend freely if the stocks are in a well-known warehouse at a large port or marketing centre. The producers' organisation under a valorisation scheme will therefore find it much easier to borrow if its members hand over their stocks to itself, and if these stocks are then stored either at large ports or at definite centres up-country under the direct control and management of the organisation or the government of the country. Granted that this is done, the producers' organisation will probably be able to borrow from the banks in the same way, and at least to the same extent, as merchants do every day—that is, up to 70–80 per cent. of the value of the stocks at the current market price. Now under the valorisation scheme, the market price in the bumper year will be the average or normal price, because only an average supply is actually being brought to market. Thus the producers' organisation will be able to borrow up to 70–80 per cent. of the average or normal price of a bag or other unit of the product, the production cost of which has been far less than normal because of the abnormally high yield of the bumper crop. In other words, the producers' organisation will probably be *able* to borrow far more than the difference between its receipts from what is sold in the bumper-crop year and the total costs of producing that bumper crop, and if it succumbs to this obvious temptation, the advantage of the valorisation scheme will be partly or wholly lost, and indeed the results may easily be worse than under the merchant-speculator regime of *laissez-faire*. And the trouble is that it will obviously find it very hard to resist such a temptation.

This is why the Brazilian coffee valorisation scheme came to such a disastrous end. The St Paulo Coffee Institute, the growers' organisation, failed to realise the absolute necessity of borrowing as little as possible. Consequently it borrowed all it could, in order to be able to give the producers the largest possible advance on the excess of the bumper crop of 1927 as it was deposited in the state warehouses. And it was able to borrow a great deal, for the banks which lent to it failed to realise that the whole conditions of lending for the purpose of financing a valorisation scheme are vitally different from the ordinary everyday conditions of lending to a merchant, under which they had hitherto transacted business. Consequently the coffee planters received advances on the bumper crop of 1927 which may be calculated at roughly double the sum necessary to cover the total costs of producing that bumper crop. As a result the planters spent all they could, and most of the rest was invested in what appeared at the time to be the most promising line of investment, namely in new or extended coffee plantations. Hence the great expansion of productive capacity, which was bound to wreck the valorisation scheme sooner or later, even if there had been no second bumper crop in 1929 following so unexpectedly quickly on the bumper crop of 1927, and even if there had been no world trade depression.

The dismal story of Brazilian coffee is therefore no argument against our general abstract conclusion in favour of the superiority of valorisation over the merchant-speculator regime: on the contrary it bears out the truth of our analysis. Brazil has, in fact, conducted an experiment of enormous importance for the producers of all crops which are subject to large variations in yield as the result of variations in the weather. The moral of the Brazilian story is not that valorisation is necessarily unsound and useless, but that all producers who conduct valorisation schemes in the future, and all bankers who assist in their finance, should learn, by the tragic and bitter experience of Brazil, the essential conditions which must be observed if valorisation is to be the success which it undoubtedly can be.

As was remarked in the Preface, this small book does not claim to be more than an interim report on a very wide subject, and it cannot be made the basis for a comprehensive and final judgment; indeed, it is as yet impossible to frame such a judgment on the basis of our existing knowledge and experience. This is not to say that no conclusions of any sort can yet be drawn: on the contrary, it is hoped that the preceding pages have shown that some important principles can be formulated, and some useful practical lessons learned, concerning several different kinds of control schemes under various conditions. The more important of these principles are summarised on pp. 216–18, 225–28 and 248–50, as shortly and definitely as the complexities of the different problems permit. But there is a great gulf between these summaries and a final and comprehensive judgment on the whole subject of artificial control, and for the latter the time is not ripe. One general and comprehensive conclusion, however, stands out from this short study, namely that there is no clear-cut issue between artificial or conscious control and so-called *laissez-faire*, because their relative merits and demerits depend upon the particular kind of control which under given circumstances is proposed as an alternative to *laissez-faire*, and how it will be administered in practice. If this book serves no other purpose than to drive home this truth and its implications, it will not have been written in vain.

INDEX

Printed in the United States
By Bookmasters